1971. 1999. WAR STORIES

AIR CMDE NITIN SATHE

Vitasta

To the Indian Armed Forces for
being the pillar of strength to
our great nation. You continue to
safeguard our frontiers.

Published by
Renu Kaul Verma
Vitasta Publishing Pvt Ltd
2/15, Ansari Road, Daryaganj
New Delhi - 110 002
info@vitastapublishing.com

ISBN: 978-93-90961-47-4

First Edition 2023
MRP ₹525

Map Courtesy: Google Maps
Edited by Alisha Verma
Editorial Support by Abhishek Rana
Typeset & Cover Design by Somesh Kumar Mishra
Printed by Vikas Computer and Printers, New Delhi

Contents

एयर चीफ मार्शल वी आर चौधरी
प वि से मे अ वि से मे वा से मे ए डी सी
Air Chief Marshal VR Chaudhari
PVSM AVSM VM ADC

Tel : (011) Off : 23012517
Res : 23017300
Fax : 23018853

वायु सेना मुख्यालय
नई दिल्ली - 110011
Air Headquarters
New Delhi - 110011

FOREWORD

1. Unadulterated, raw and real anecdotes from the soldiers who have toiled hard in wars always evoke immediate interest and patriotic fervour amongst its readers.

2. Contribution of IAF in the outcome of 1971 war and the Kargil conflict needs no special emphasis, but the vivid depiction of war scenes by the author Air Cmde Nitin Sathe in the book deserves a suitable mention.

3. Personal stories of both the wars are culled from personal interviews conducted by the author over many years. These stories from the war veterans offer a glimpse into the minds of those who made decisions at the right time that changed the course of history. Each story evinces leadership, motivation, man & machine management and most importantly, the resilience and perseverance of our soldiers. The book brings out many aspects of operations carried out at the icy heights of Kargil and the muddy landing grounds of East Pakistan and is an amazing compilation of first hand experiences.

4. I am confident that this book would be a great source of inspiration and awe to all the readers. My best wishes to the editorial team.

Jai Hind!

Air Chief Marshal
Chief of the Air Staff

23 Sep 22

SECTION ONE

THE FIGHT FOR LIBERATION

INTRODUCTION

IN 1947, Pakistan was trying to handle a difficult partition with India. It was a country split into two parts called West and East Pakistan at a distance of 1,500 km apart, with the giant landmass of India in between. Right from the time they gained independence, it was clear to the Pakistani leadership that keeping the country together as one was a difficult proposition, for many reasons more than the physical distance between the two parts.

The power centre of this country lay in the West, and the command and control over the East which had more than 55 per cent of the total population, was difficult. A population which thought itself so different than their western counterparts that it always felt alienated and treated like a second-rate citizen.

The genetic and ethnic origin of the people was different, they led different lifestyles, had different customs and thought processes. And of course, their politics and political ideals were totally different too. Their histories, geographies and all that constitutes demography differed so much that the two stood apart as chalk and cheese. The only thing in common was the religion, but this too was followed differently.

The treatment meted out to the local eastern population over the years led to a gradual unrest, blowing up into a political struggle for independence. Faced with the danger of one more partition, the leaders of the West decided to go in for a severe course of action, which included taking over control by the military, mass arrest of 'anti-nationals,' politicians and bigwigs, and subduing the entire country by the rule of the gun. As it naturally happens in such cases, the military went on a rampage and mass rapes, lootings and killings ensued, pushing the eastern state to the brink of a civil war.

Terrorised and homeless, a disturbed population fled in hordes towards the west, pouring into India in millions. India, in those days, was an economically backward state, just about managing to stand on its feet, and could ill afford to look after this refugee population. The influx grew with each passing day, throwing the entire state machinery out of gear.

Intervention and meddling with another country's

internal problems was never an intent, but this crisis was hurting India deep, both in the short and long terms. The Indians needed to take action. Help to the freedom struggle began, and we finally got sucked into the war which created Bangladesh.

To ease off the pressure in the east and the imminent war around the corner, Pakistan decided to open up on the western front with a pre-emptive attack on seven Indian Air Force bases on 3 December 1971. What followed is history written by many—discussed threadbare.

I was barely seven years old in 1971, but carry vivid memories of the war. My father, an artillery officer, became a part of the liberation struggle in May 1971, when he and his guns were clandestinely taken into East Pakistan and deployed in support of the Mukti Bahini. After the war, he got on with his life in the Army, and 1971 came up for discussions only over a drink when he met up with his old friends who had fought alongside him. I am sure he had a horde of stories to tell, some of which he told us at bedtime. When I took to write them and wanted him to describe the war to me in detail, he was too old to remember. He met his end in December 2014, and much of history, sadly, was confined to the flames with him. Sometimes, I feel awful about it.

I realised that I needed to get the stories of the war—yet untold from the veterans and got busy connecting with Daddy's comrades. In a few years from now, these gallant grand old soldiers would have finished their tenure on earth and the unwritten history may die with them. Having got in touch with a few of them, my endeavour is to get you as many short and sweet 'untold' stories that I can in the chapters of this book.

As I set about writing this book, my intention was to speak to as many veterans as I could to get out some unwritten aspects of the war of '71. Some veterans going strong at the age of 80 and more, could still recall from memory and tell me a few stories. I shall forever remain thankful to them all. I must admit I have more in this basket on '71, which I am still researching on. Maybe in my next book, I shall get you more fascinating stories of the 1971 war.

Here it goes!

BLACK OUTS AND TELEGRAM

COL BK SATHE

This story is about my father Colonel BK Sathe, fondly remembered as 'BK' by his friends.

The siren wailed once again. It was early evening of December 20—my father's birthday, my sister's had been a day earlier. We had a quiet celebration at home. Dad was missed, this was one of the few times that he had not been present for his daughter's birthday. From wherever he was posted, he would invariably pay us a surprise visit during the last days of the year, getting us many interesting presents, and of course, chocolates.

This time, however, he was fighting the war.

The '71 war was over by 20 December and the entire country was celebrating a resounding victory.

The photographs of the signing of the Instrument of Surrender of 16 December had been flashed on the front pages of all newspapers. But for us, it still appeared to be dragging on with air raid sirens wailing a few times during the day as well as night. We had been taught to run to the corner, face the wall and stand there till the 'all safe' siren went off—signaling that the threat had passed. I remember going into hiding, often under the sofa, in the living room since I found it an interesting place to pass time with my toy rifle!

The logic, as we understood it then, was that if a bomb was to strike the house, we would be safe from the falling debris. But no bombs fell anywhere near where we were at Deolali in Maharashtra, staying at the separated family quarters while our fathers fought the enemy on the front.

The siren had wailed yet again and I had gone under cover in my favourite place.

As the all clear siren went off, the doorbell rang and we looked at each other. Who could it be walking around in the open with the threat of an air raid, we wondered. Beyond the open door, stood a postman in his crisp khaki uniform with his side-cap perilously dangling from his head, 'Telegram!' he announced. My mother went white in the face and sat down on the floor as soon as she heard the word.

Just the other day, she and her friends had gone to pray at the temple to thank god for the safety of their husbands after the surrender was signed. As they returned, they saw some commotion at the Kulkarni's residence. The postman had just delivered a telegram about the sad demise of Major Kulkarni on the eastern front.

We, the three children, looked at each other wondering what had led to mummy collapsing in a heap whilst our grandmother and house help rushed to help Mummy to her feet. As they struggled to get her up, she whispered, 'Open it' or words to that effect. Her words moved something in us. We realized the enormity of the situation. The telegram could contain news that would change the rest of our lives.

The telegram had been the harbinger of bad news throughout the war and this could be just it.

After passing the small piece of paper all around, no one had the courage to tear it open. Finally, it was the postman who volunteered to do it for us.

'Happy Birthday Neelima!' he announced reading from the small piece of paper.

'Why didn't the censors open these telegrams too and send them to us?' my mother had remarked rather sarcastically after we had relaxed back into normalcy. A few months earlier, one of Dad's letters to her on the special 'Military Inland Letter' had been opened and some lines obliterated with white ink. Thereafter, all letters from the 'front' from dad had arrived opened and with a big stamp 'CENSORED' across the top.

It took a few minutes for the shock of the telegram to dissipate and the smiles returned to our faces. Mummy looked up to the skies and thanked god for the good news, or rather, for dad's safety. Dad had been promoted during the war and was to take over as Commanding Officer of a 'new raising' (New Regiment) very soon. In fact, he was to move out of the eastern front and be with us on his way to the new location.

My sister had just turned 12 and my brother and I were still hovering in single digits. The only thing we knew of the war was the siren which brought our world to a standstill. We had also keenly participated in the 'blackout' exercise of pasting newspapers on all the glass windows of our home so that no light would filter out during the night. It was as if the Paki Air Force was just waiting for us to give our position away and bomb us to smithereens!

Other than that, it was business as usual at Deolali—with school in the morning, homework and play in the evening.

Daddy operated in the eastern theatre in 1971. He was the second-in-command of the 'Mountain Regiment' which had the 75/24 pounder British guns, called the 25 Pounder by the British and used extensively in the Second World War. This gun had been modified and refurbished by the DRDO in the '60s and called the 'Packed Howitzer.'

'The 75/24 could fire at low and high angles unlike the old British version making it ideal for the mountains,' remarks veteran, Brig Gharpure, who fought on the western front. Once we acquired the 105 mm Indian Field Gun, the 75/24 was taken off service and was soon basking in museums and as a roadside display in cantonments.

I remember dad describing to me how the 75/24 guns could be broken up into parts in a jiffy, and could be carried by three *khacchars* (mules) to the new place of deployment. This mobility gave the artillery increased survivability. The enemy gun locating radars took time to find out where the artillery fire was coming from and while they did their trigonometry, the guns had already been moved away to safety! The range of the gun was just about 9 km and was ideal to be deployed alongside the infantry fighting in the mountains. Although it was a vintage design, the *topchi's* (Artillery men like to be called that) of yesteryears swear by this gun. It was accurate, highly mobile and almost maintenance free, my father had told me.

Dad had sneaked into East Pakistan well before the war had started for the reconnaissance of the terrain on the other side. He had disguised himself as a co-driver of a truck laden with goods and traveled into East Pakistan to be received by the underground fighters of the Mukti Bahini (Vahini). He operated in and out of East Pakistan right from the May of 1971 till the actual declaration of ceasefire and came back to India soon after the surrender was signed.

Now, publically known, India was indeed involved in arming and training the freedom fighters of East Pakistan. Dad was a part of this effort, although he didn't divulge much about it even after he retired. A few years before he passed away, he did try and remember what had happened but I think it was too late. So, some of his stories were extracted out of his unit officers who fought alongside him.

He did describe, in his jovial manner, how he had grown a beard, learnt a spattering of Bangla, was comfortable wearing his *lungi* and learnt to live off the land in the absence of any ration supply. He once also told me how he had enjoyed eating a snake, which he said, tasted just like fish. From what I have been able to discern from his unit, some of the Indian artillery was inducted into the hills of East Pakistan well before the war had begun to help the Mukti Bahini fight the war.

Yet, there is one incident that daddy oft repeated to his grandchildren which went something like this, 'I was leading a recce mission through the jungles in heavy thundershower. It was imperative that we got to the next point as we navigated through the marsh and swampy earth through the darkness of the night…'

His team had taken a momentary break behind

a big rock. Dad handed his weapon to his buddy and went some thirty feet ahead to look at what lay on the other side of the high ground. Within a minute or two of his walking away, a bolt of lightning struck very close, making him jump out of his skin. Looking back, he was aghast to see that the soldier who had held his weapon had been reduced to ashes. Two of his boys in the team were dead. They completed the last rites of their fallen brothers at the site itself and moved on through the rain and lightning to their destination. Later, every time my father heard peals of thunder and saw lightening, he was reminded of this unfortunate incident and how he was saved by a whisker on that fateful day in the jungles of East Pakistan.

Brig Gharpure, who is 85 now and was a good friend of dad, narrated me his account of the war on the western front.

'At that time we were just Captains and Majors and did not understand the "strategy" part of the war. We were at the "fighting" end and not the "thinking" end of the war at that time!' he quipped to me.

My father had reached Dacca with his men and guns a few days before the signing of the Instrument of Surrender and was enjoying the joys of the liberation with his new found Bengali friends. An army friend from those times, a retired General, narrated how Daddy drove through the war-torn roads of Dacca in his open Jeep.

'He used to drive fast through the town and behave as if the Indian Army owned the town! Friendly with many locals, he found help at hand whenever he required it in the capital city,' he narrated to me.

On 19 December, he had gone to the local post office and sent us the telegram, not thinking what consternation it would cause, at least till the time the flap was torn open at our end!

Daddy was airlifted from the Dacca airport on 21 December in a Caribou aircraft. He stepped on Indian soil in Calcutta the same day. He was moving to take over as the first Commanding Officer of a newly formed Medium Regiment, which was to operate with the recently acquired Russian 130 mm guns. His unit was to be formed out of soldiers who had been drawn out of a unit which had been all but decimated during the war.

A few days later he was with us, a war wizened father who was all set to 'command' a new set of people.

PRIMITIVE EARLY WARNING

BRIG MV GHARPURE

Brig MV Gharpure, IC 8612, 85 years of age, better known as 'Bhau' (meaning Brother), retired from the Army many years ago and is now settled in Pune. He and my Dad were good friends from Artillery and I often heard Dad and Gharpure Sir taunting each other about their roles in the war of 1971. While dad was a 'Field Gunner,' Gharpure was an Air Defence man.

As I was preparing to leave for my Services Selection Board (SSB) interview as a budding 15 year-old, it was Brig Gharpure who had briefed me for the same. He was intrigued as to why I was choosing to join the IAF and not my Dad's regiment. The only words of advice that he gave me on a cold wintry day in Jammu before I left for the railway station were, 'Go and enjoy the process of selection. I am sure you will pass and do your Dad and us proud!'

Brig Gharpure has very vivid memories of the war which he narrated to me.

'In '71, I was just a Major with 13 years of service and an Air Defence Battery Commander which was part of the 152 AD regiment.' Detached from his unit, he was to operate independently during the war. With just five junior officers who were mere rookies, the task was daunting, to say the least.

'By the July of 1971, the training courses undertaken at the Deolali Cantonment were stopped and officers returned to their units to augment the strength for the impending war. By the next month, a large number of senior officers visited the station to meet the troops and it was clear that something was off. This, along with the fact that at the political level, Mrs Indira Gandhi had paid a visit to many countries to garner support for the war made us quite sure that war was indeed a possibility soon,' says the veteran.

MOVING TO THE FRONT

'There was no clarity when and where we would be headed, but the ammunition trains started arriving in September which involved a lot of hard work. One day, a consignment of sand tires arrived and we were told to change the tires of all our vehicles. This gave us a fair idea that we were headed somewhere into the desert (Rajasthan) sector. We were ordered to be ready to move at a short notice, and in the interim, we continued to train ourselves at our home base. One by one, units around us suddenly left for unknown destinations,' remembers Gharpure.

'Soon, it was our turn. The special train arrived and we were loaded up within two days. The first casualty of war happened during the loading itself. One of the men who was using a crane to load the heavy equipment was electrocuted by the overhead DC cables and died instantly. This was not a good start to the war, there was a pall of gloom when we left Deolali at night a couple of days later,' remembers Gharpure. 'No ladies came to see us off, but the band played some marching tunes as we chugged out of the station which made us feel a little better.'

'The driver of the train only knew what was his next destination for change of engine that's all!' says the Brigadier. 'We had a first-class bogie for just the five of us. Before we knew it, we were in Mumbai, from where we changed to the western line and headed towards Barmer.'

They reached Barmer around midnight and it was time to go and meet the Brigade Commander to receive orders.

Just then, his second-in-command came to him with a unique problem. His young deputy had loaded his entire office along with the furniture and a lot of rum in one of the wagons that were of no use in the field conditions. 'He had even got some picture portraits and potted plants which adorned my office in Deolali!' remembers the old man.

The young officer had been over-enthusiastic to ensure that his boss was comfortable in the field, and had not realised that most of the paraphernalia wasn't required in war! He was promptly asked to send the extras back to Deolali where the rake was headed to get another unit.

The Air Defence unit operated the vintage L/60 gun developed well before the Second World War. Produced by the Swedish, the Germans were the first to use it during the war, albeit not widely. It was towed by a vehicle and had a manual sight only, unlike the L/70 which was radar controlled and had a better rate of fire. 'With a shortage of the L/70, we had no choice but to continue the use of the L/60 in the war, especially in our sector. Since it was an all-manual operation, the crew had to be extremely well trained. Our crew was extremely good and integrated well as a team,' remembers Gharpure.

'We were deployed alongside the units of the 11 Infantry Division. There was no formalised Control and Reporting System (C&R System) and we had the rudimentary reports coming from forward located troops as well as through the railway communication systems, wherein the railway station masters had been trained to pass information of enemy aircraft when seen. The only real information came from our own observation posts located around 5 km around our guns, and this early warning was hardly adequate!'

'Despite all the limitations, my battery can boast of one enemy aircraft kill and we took back parts of the wreckage as a memento of the war.'

'Our Air Force aircraft were operating further north and south of where we were. So, any aircraft that ventured into our air space was enemy. Thankfully, there was no chance of committing fratricide and no problems in Identification of Friend or Foe (IFF),' quips the octogenarian.

THE EARLY WARNING SYSTEM

'During the war, we reached as far as almost 40 km into Pakistan on the Munabao-Khokropar axis. We held on to the territory and the logistics was stretched to the limit. The engineers had done a good job of making duckboard tracks through the desert so that the supplies could reach us. Rather than using these "duckboard" tracks, I preferred travelling in my jeep on the railway track! There was no rail traffic, and it was interesting to stop at the small abandoned two or three stations en route.'

'I remember, one day, we decided to explore some

locked rooms at one of the stations during my drive to Khokhropar. I first told my JCO to look for booby traps and then got the big padlocks opened that denied us entry. We were quite surprised to find stacks of Bank of Pakistan cheque books in one of the rooms. On yet another journey, we discovered a large number of boxes of condoms!' recalls Gharpure with a chuckle.

The Indian Railways had opened up the railway line ahead of Gadra Road into Pakistan and there were plans of running freight trains right up to the unit location at Khokhropar. 'I remember one afternoon when a trainload of ammunition arrived at Khokhropar. We were immediately ordered to provide Air Defence support to it, should an attack materialise. And an attack did materialise that day!'

'The enemy aircraft came in from the setting sun, which made observation difficult in the first round of attack. My gunner was aiming at the approaching aircraft and let off a volley of lead. One of the rockets from the enemy aircraft hit this man who died with his hand on the trigger. The rockets also managed to hit one of the wagons full of ammunition and the explosions started. My brave JCO still managed to get to the gun, sit on top of the dead man and fired at the attacking aircraft till they melted away into the darkness.'

The dead gunner was given an in-situ cremation but they had a larger problem at hand. Fire had to be prevented from spreading to the other railway wagons and they went around searching for the engine driver who had gone into hiding once the air attack came in.

'The driver found, we then managed to uncouple the rest of the train from the burning wagon and moved it by about a kilometre from the siding, preventing further damage. The engine driver was petrified at first but we sent one man with a machine gun along with him to give him some kind of reassurance.'

This was the second casualty of the war and the ashes were taken back to the boy's village in Maharashtra after the funeral.

The railways were quick to acknowledge the bravery of the engine driver, and he was awarded the equivalent of a Vir Chakra and a plot of land by the Railways.

Gharpure also had a hand in improvising an early warning system by getting direct access to the communication system of the railways. The Indian Railways, even at that time had a large communication network spread all over India in a zonal manner. The system could be of use for early warning. Without early warning, the effectiveness of our Air Defence dropped by 70 per cent at least.

'I was initially based at a small railway station. I observed that the station master could speak to all stations in Rajasthan without hindrance just by saying "Hello Jodhpur, Hello Barmer." I had a discussion with him and requested him to give my Command Post a connection on this line. He readily agreed. I then spoke to Munabao, Jodhpur and Barmer station masters and requested them to inform Gadra Road if any aircraft flew over them towards this side. I carried this line and their telephones (funny looking gadgets they were!) and extended their line to Khokhropar once the railway line got extended. It turned out to be a limited but effective means of early warning,' says the Brigadier.

'We also did an improvisation of sorts by having our guns mounted on the wagons of the trains that were getting us food and water. It was much like the Second World War movies like *Von Ryans Express*. Flat top wagons were attached at both ends of trains and we mounted one gun each atop them to provide protection in their journey into the Pakistani-held territory.'

There was really no time to think as the war progressed. And before they knew—it was over! Gharpure's unit, however, continued to stay inside Pakistani-held territory and went on with their training till withdrawal was ordered.

Gharpure Sir shared another incident of the war with me. With the two casualties taking place and the bombs falling around, there was a young soldier who became delirious and wanted to go back home. He wailed and sobbed through the night and this was detrimental to the morale of the troops.

'In war, a soldier can be shot for not adhering to

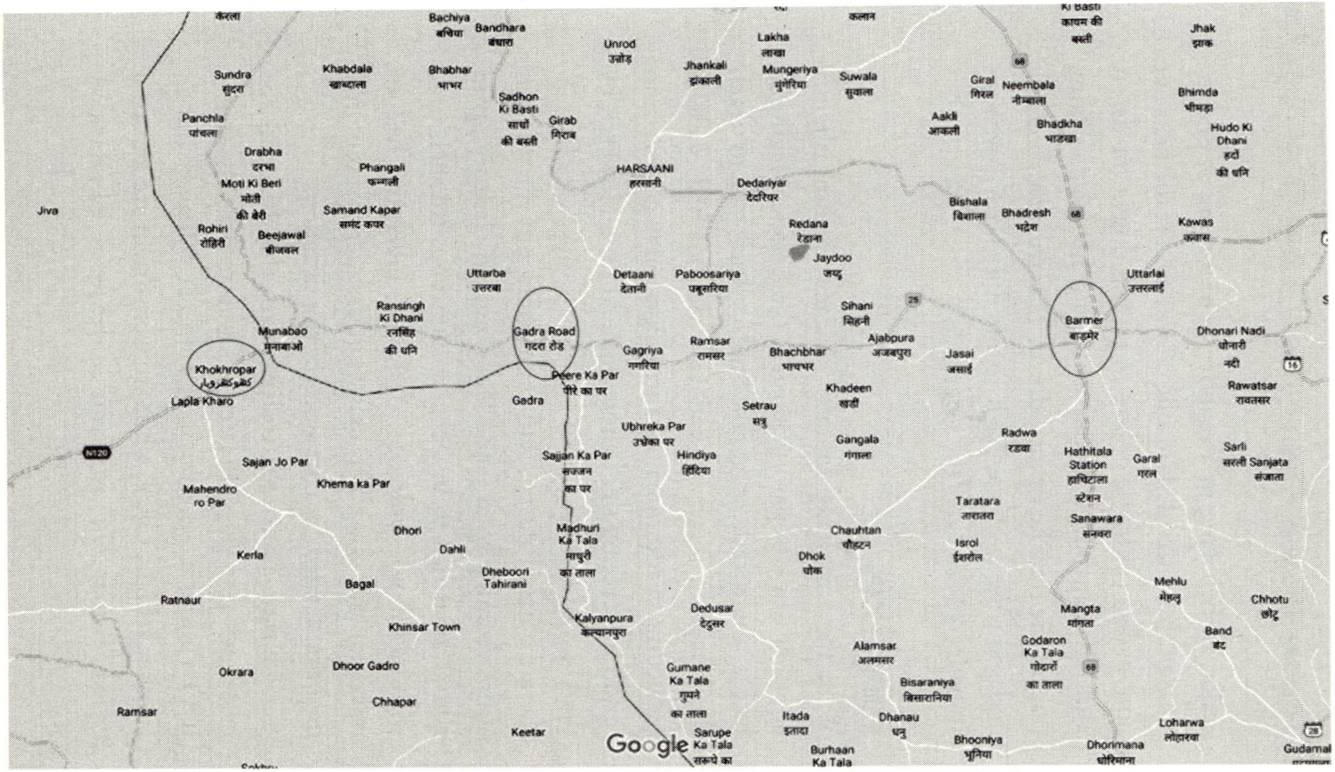

Representation of Khokhropar, Gadra Road and Barmer on Map.

orders or behaving in a manner unbecoming of one for treason. But I decided on a novel way to sort the man out and made an example of him. A pit was dug in the desert and the man buried under sand with his head sticking out till the time he calmed down. This trick worked well and soon the boy was back to his duty. Fear psychosis spreads like fire!' says the veteran.

A NARROW ESCAPE

With the advancing Infantry Brigade reaching slightly ahead of Khokhropar in Pakistan, the Engineer regiment had a tough task at hand. The logistics had to reach the troops in the front and Gen Bewoor had plans of inducting an additional Infantry Division to go deep into Sindh by severing the Lahore-Karachi link. However, by the time additional forces could be brought to bear in the area, East Pakistan had capitulated and the war was almost coming to an end. The occupied territory up to Khokhropar had to be held by the troops till such time withdrawal was ordered. Therefore, Gharpure had to travel up and down this axis quite frequently even after hostilities ended, to take stock of the situation.

'I always preferred to drive with the driver in the passenger seat since the terrain was tricky. My senior JCO (Junior Commissioned Officer) followed me in another vehicle. Once, while we were driving to a feature called "Parbat Ali," we came under an aerial attack. A rocket went clean through the chest of my driver, Shinde and through the rear floor of the open jeep. Thankfully, it did not explode and I was saved. My jeep was still roadworthy and I asked the JCO in the following jeep to carry out the last rites of the boy back at the unit HQ and join me later.'

'The news of death is indeed one of the painful things of war. The ashes of Shinde were sent in an urn to his family and were taken by one of the senior JCOs of the unit. I was quite fond of Shinde and he had been with me for a while. He had just become a father a few days ago. Losing men in war is part of the game and we had to take it in our stride.'

THE VIPS COME CALLING

I asked the veteran to go back in time and give me some more interesting anecdotes of the war. He thought for a while and started another narration.

'Sometime in the last week of November (before the action started), we were asked to come to Barmer for an important meeting. The officers gathered under a clump of trees and waited for the Brigade Commander to arrive. In a fancy looking Jonga which did not look military like at all, came a man in a specially tailored "different" looking uniform with the rank of a Colonel on his shoulders.'

They were all pleasantly surprised. It was the Maharaja

of Jaipur, Colonel Bhawani Singh with his ADC who had come to meet them. 'What a handsome and upright man and what a colorful uniform he wore!' reminisces Gharpure. While Col Bhawani sat down next to the GoC, the then Chief of the Army Staff (COAS), Gen Sam Manekshaw and Lt Gen Bewoor, the Commander-in-Chief drove in. The officers had not expected to meet so many VIPs at one place for this special meeting and it surely lifted their spirits to be with them over tea.

Gen Sam Manekshaw didn't waste time, he gave a short and sweet speech which went thus:

> *Gentlemen,*
> *We are at war! I propose to finish it soon, but till then, you all will ensure that we strike hard at our enemy. I will not accept any shortcomings or cowardice. I have ordered your Army Commander, Bewoor, to ensure that you and the troops under your command are well supplied.*
> *Best of luck!*
> *Happy Shooting!*

Gen Bewoor was the Commander-in-Chief (GoC-in-C) of Southern Command based at Jodhpur. Around November end, Gharpure received a call from his GoC that the Army Commander wanted to visit the unit commanded by one 'Bhau.'

'Who is this *Bhau*?' asked the GoC. When Gharpure replied that Bhau was indeed him, the GoC said, 'Oh! It is you, is it? I should have known! One *tantya* (Maharashtrians are called 'tantyas' in the army) wants to meet another!' he remarked jokingly. After enquiring, if he had the logistics to look after the VIP guest, the GoC left it to Bhau to look after the big boss.

'We were housed in the PWD guest house right opposite the Gadra Road railway station. We used to cook some dishes for ourselves and augment it with the food from the 'langar' (the mess for the men). But more needed to be done for the visiting VIP.'

'The guest house was vacated for the General's visit and we decided to cook for him ourselves.' Bewoor was pleasantly surprised to be treated to a sumptuous lunch consisting of Clear Chicken Soup, Chicken-a la Kiev, Mashed Potatoes and Baked Spinach and to top it all, Chocolate ice-cream and chocolates for dessert.

And while they were resting in the early hours of the night, a loud bang was heard. 'We heard enemy aircrafts returning west after striking the airbase at Barmer. It was 2 December, and the first of the pre-emptive strikes from Pakistan had gone through to strike Barmer.'

As he heard the loud bangs, Bewoor ran out of his tent shouting at the gunners on duty. '******** why don't you shoot the ******* using the choicest expletives in Marathi. After things became silent, Gharpure went to

Bewoor and explained the limitations of his guns.

The aircraft that struck Barmer had been well out of range, and if they had fired, their own position would have been given away with the patterned tracers lighting the sky. The Army Commander was happy with the explanation and gave a *shabash* to Gharpure. Soon, Bewoor was on his way to supervise operations from his own HQ at Jodhpur.

By this time, I was so interested in the stories he was telling that I couldn't help but fish for more. The veteran Brigadier did not disappoint.

WOMEN AND WAR

'Our rear party consisted of two jawans and 96 separated families. My wife, just 25 years of age with two little children was the leader of the pack and took charge of the lot.' She had to see that they were looked after in the absence of their husbands who were braving the bullets and fighting the enemy.

At the end of the month, she was told that many of the families had run out of money. Taking charge of the situation, she decided to pay a visit to the local bank manager. 'We had about 2000 Rupees in my account but the manager agreed to give her an overdraft of 19,000 Rupees so that all the families could be given about Rupees 200 each to sustain them for a few days. 'She assured the manager that the money would be returned as soon as I sent it to her from wherever I was!' the veteran tells me.

Having collected the money, the distribution was arranged in a typical military fashion. Lists were made and the ladies lined up to receive the money and put their thumb impressions against their names. This list was promptly sent to the front along with one of the jawans who was proceeding to the front post his leave.

'It took almost two months to collect money from our boys and send it to the bank. The bank manager was very kind, he did not charge me interest for this overdraft and thanked me for being prompt in returning the money which he had given at his own risk!'

The families had other problems too. Often there were rumours that there was shortage of food and water for the soldiers and that their living conditions were pitiable. This was also compounded by some of the wives receiving letters from their husbands who told them that they had no time to shave and wrote things like 'I don't know if I will return home in one piece or, if you will be able to recognize me in the state that I am in!'

This kind of communication did not do well to the ladies and families of the soldiers. It led to a fair amount of anguish and tears in the living quarters. 'It was my wife who went around the camp and pacified them, despite the fact that she too was as afraid as any of them,' says Gharpure.

Distressed by all the rumour mongering, Mrs

Gharpure decided to make a call to her husband with some of the wives in tow. There was a civilian telephone supervisor in the Military Exchange at that time by the name of Pathak. He requested her to come to the nearest military telephone at 1800 hrs that evening. He then managed to hook up a call to Gharpure from Deolali to Gadra Road, connected through multiple exchanges at Mumbai, Pune, Delhi, Jodhpur and Barmer. 'The line obviously was faint and one could barely make out who was at the other end of the line,' remembers the veteran.

'Luckily, my driver Shinde was with me that day and his wife was available at the other end. We made them speak to each other and he told her that there was no need to worry and all was well with everyone.' Shinde told his wife, 'We are inside Pakistan (Khokrapar) and are very comfortable. We get chicken to eat every day, fresh milk and a tot of rum as and when we need it.'

'Things cooled down to a large extent with this communication', says the Brigadier.

LIFE AND WAR

Brig Gharpure narrated another happy, yet sad incident which took place in the 'rear' which brings out the camaraderie and bonhomie amongst the families. 'One evening, one of the ladies came panting home to tell my wife that a lady was in labour and needed help.'

'Gunner Shinde's wife is in agony ma'am, we need to

get her to hospital!' she said. Mrs Gharpure quickly drove out in her Standard Herald car to pick up the lady and get her to the hospital. 'There were so many volunteers who wanted to get into the car to accompany Mrs Shinde to hospital!' remembers the veteran. A brief tussle and discussions later, three of the ladies managed to get into the small confines of the car and off they went to the hospital. A baby boy was born to the soldier who was fighting at the front.

There were celebrations and sweets all around the camp and the good news brought more cheer amongst all the ladies!

After the new addition, it was decided that Shinde would be brought back home and another soldier would replace him instead so that he could get a chance to see his new born son.

Sadly, it were his ashes which arrived a few days later.

Such is life and such is war. No matter how hard you try, not everything goes to plan.

'As a Commanding Officer, during my stay with my troops in this war, I learnt that it is necessary to ensure that the "rear" is kept happy and away from rumours arising out of mail from youngsters fighting the war.'

'The 1971 war was a success indeed. The operations was extremely well-planned, well-administered, and carried out by well-motivated soldiers, and well-controlled at all levels of Command. We never once felt neglected, since all Commanders were always available and supportive, and open to suggestions. I never felt scared of any of my seniors in the theatre of operation,' remarks the Brigadier.

'My only recommendation is that our system of honouring the brave and recommending the bravery on paper to the highest authority in writing is flawed. It needs serious thought and a change,' concluded the veteran.

***

I paid my gratitude to the Brigadier for all the stories that he had wonderfully narrated to me.

Once upon a time, as a child, this was the man I addressed as 'Uncle.' Now, we both are veterans and I address him as Sir!

It's all a matter of time!

FIRST SHOTS FIRED

My association with this veteran goes back a long way. Although he was very senior to me, we spent many an interesting hour together in and out of the cockpit over the years. Calling him brilliant in flying and academics would be an understatement, but the only problem with this man was that he loved, and still loves to remain out of the spotlight!

Post-retirement and out of the cockpit, his quest for knowledge only increased manifold and it was not long before he became a history wizard of sorts. With dates and names at his fingertips, he could rattle out stories of the Montgomery's, Rommel's and Shivaji's. He also researched adequately on the many wars that India has fought in recent times.

Some of the anecdotes of the old man are difficult

to comprehend and digest, but he always backs them up with proof and references, you simply have to believe what he says! Prepared for a soak and swim in the sea of knowledge, he is always ready with a tale or two for you. Ask him a question and he delves into his memory (which he claims is fading!) and in a few seconds you hear fascinating tales from history.

And that is exactly what happened. I was researching for this book that I was contemplating on writing, and decided to call 'the guru' as I would like to call him, for information. As he stared talking, I was ready with my pencil and paper to scribble and absorb as much as I could. In the next hour or so, he left me spellbound with a captivating story which allowed me to write this chapter. This is just the tip of the iceberg. I wish I could spend more time with him.

As he started his monologue, punctuated only by exclamations from my side, he first quoted from Mrs Indira Gandhi's speech to the nation made on 3 December 1971 when she formally declared war on Pakistan—the second time in her tenure as the Prime Minister.

'This is relevant to what I am going to say subsequently,' he says.

> *I speak to you at a moment of grave peril to our country and our people. Some hours ago, soon after 5.30 pm on 3 December, Pakistan launched a full*

scale war against us.

The Pakistan Air Force suddenly struck at our airfields in Amritsar, Pathankot, Srinagar, Avantipur, Utterlai, Jodhpur, Ambala, and Agra.

Their ground forces are shelling our defence positions in Sulemankhi, Khemkaran, Poonch, and other sectors.

Since last March, we have borne the heaviest of burdens and withstood the greatest of pressure and a tremendous effort to urge the world to help in bringing about a peaceful solution.

Today, the war in Bangladesh has become a war on India, and this imposes upon me, my government, and the people of India an awesome responsibility. We have no other option but to put our country on a war footing. Our brave officers and jawans are at their posts, mobilised for the defence of the country. Emergency has been declared. We are prepared for any eventualities.

I have no doubt that it is the united will of our people that this wanton and unprovoked aggression of Pakistan should be decisively and finally repelled. In this resolve, the government is assured of the full and unflinching support of all political parties and every Indian citizen.

We must be prepared for a long period of hardship and sacrifice. We are a peace-loving people, but we know that peace cannot last if we do not guard our freedom, our democracy, and our way of life. So today, we fight not merely for territorial integrity but for the basic ideals which have given strength to this country, and in this alone, we can progress to a better future. Aggression must be met, and the people of India will meet it with fortitude and determination, with discipline and the utmost unity.

All India Radio had to wait to make this recording public almost till the midnight of 3 December, he explains. The Prime Minister was waiting for a green signal from the east.

Exiled Pakistani Bengali pilots trained by the IAF, flew an Indian Air Force helicopter and transport plane that had been hastily modified for delivering armament from airfields in the eastern part of our country. They fired the first shots at targets in East Pakistan on the night of 3 December. As soon as the news of the safe recovery of the aircraft after a successful mission reached Delhi, as if on cue, the speech made by Mrs Gandhi went on air, and the war was declared formally. The clouds of this impending war had been looming large from the beginning of the year itself.

The exiled Pakistani Bengali pilots were trained by our IAF at several bases located along the eastern border of the country. 'Kilo Flight' as it was called, was a small part of the larger 'Kilo Force' formed out of a large population of East Pakistanis fleeing their country into India.

This story recounts how we trained the East Pakistani refugees inside Indian camps run by our Armed Forces. These men and women, thereafter, went back into their country and assisted the Mukti Bahini to fight the oppression by the West Pakistani rulers.

'But before we get to know more about the Kilo Flight, it would be pertinent to know how the Kilo Force was formed, and we need to go back in time,' said my Guru to me as the chat warmed up.

In early 1971, Sheikh Mujibur Rehman (who later came to be called the Father of the Nation) announced on Chittagong radio that East Pakistan was separating from the control of the West and a new country was to be formed. He was trying to garner as much local support as he could within and outside of the Armed Forces deployed in East Pakistan. At that time, a fair percentage of Muslim Bangla officers and men served in the Pakistani Army, and were longing to help the cause.

A general revolt followed, after which the Pak army launched 'Operation Searchlight' to crack down on the dissidents and cleanse the 'rot.' A lot has been written and discussed about how this tragedy of 'cleansing'—rape and murder was unleashed, spreading like wildfire through the length and breadth of the country. This was the cause for the mass exodus of the population into India, a problem which our country could not afford to handle, mainly for economic reasons.

The first people to run for their lives were the officials and bureaucrats manning the various government departments, and they were accompanied by some of the soldiers of the Armed Forces, who were of Bengali origin. Although the shortest route to India was to come westwards towards Calcutta, it was found easier to escape by penetrating the porous border further east, around Agartala.

So, we had a large number of dissidents coming in and out of the country, 40 odd VIP dissidents were picked up and taken to Calcutta. These formed the core group of the Government-in-exile, and were housed in a building named Ramkutir in Tollygunj near the Hoogly. The army signal unit located alongside provided them the much-needed security.

'Mind you, there were a lot of Pakistani *jasoos*'(enemy agents) in Calcutta then, whose task was to eliminate these so-called traitors,' says the veteran.

'And do you want to hear an interesting story of Ramkutir?'

Without hearing a yes from me, he starts, 'The first HQ of Eastern Air Command under Air Vice Marshal Kundan Lal Sondhi was located in this building somewhere in 1958-59. It was originally the house of

William O'Shaughnessy—the inventor and chemist. William made batteries using clay pots and was the first to demonstrate a working telegraph using Morse Code between Diamond Point to Prinsep Ghats in 1851 for regulating the shipping on the Hooghly river. Within the next five years, the telegraph was extended from Calcutta to Peshawar, and also across the oceans to the US, Europe, and even Russia.'

Shaughnessy died a pauper because he did not realise the value of his invention and did not patent it! The East India Company took over this building in 1854 and made it the telegraph hub of India. It was, and still is the hub of telecommunication connecting the eastern most parts of our country to the mainland till date. Re-christened 'Ranikutir,' it houses a telephone exchange today.

Coming back to the story, although a loose outfit of a Bangladesh Government-in-exile was formed at Calcutta, many in Lutyens Delhi wanted it to be located at the Indian capital to have better political command and control.

But Calcutta had close proximity to Dacca not only in distance, but also in language and political thinking, and therefore, the Bangladeshi 'defectors' felt quite at home there.

There were two outstanding officers from the Pakistani forces who had defected to India in the first lot of 40 who were the backbone of the rebel movement which was picking up by mid-1971. They were Col MAG Osmani and Wg Cdr Abdul Karim Khandker (spelt Khondker on some websites), his deputy. Besides them, we also had civil servants and powerful politicians like Tajuddin Ahmed, Nazrul Islam, Mansoor Ali, and Qamruzzaman who worked tirelessly manning various portfolios of the Government-in-exile. Some of these men were arrested and murdered in the 1975 uprising in which Sheikh Mujib and his family were assassinated.

Osmani was soon sent back into Bangladesh. He had a good local following and was tasked to start the resistance movement.

Khandker was starting to work out strategies to deal with the Pakistani Army in East Pakistan and asked to create a fighting force by recruiting able-bodied men and training them at the ten odd camps set up along the eastern border to India.

A distinguished fighter pilot, Khandker had been the head of the Air Force Academy in West Pakistan earlier. He was appointed as the Deputy Chief of the Bangladesh Air Force during the war and later on, the mantle of the CAS. Post the formation of Bangladesh, he was one of the first recipients of the 'Bir Uttom,' the country's highest gallantry award. Post-retirement, he became the planning minister before retiring from public life in the '90s.

There were frequent meetings with the hoi-polloi and the political bigwigs in Delhi in the ensuing months, including meeting the PM Mrs Indira Gandhi. 'Do you know, Mrs Gandhi had five special advisors chosen from the Dogra Brahmin community of Kashmir to help her take decisions expeditiously?' my guru says in passing.

The idea of providing guerrilla training to the Bangladeshis in exile was finally accepted amidst skepticism that we should not end up arming the Bangla dissidents so heavily that they become a problem for us to handle at a later stage. The requirement at that time was to create enough trouble for the Pakistani Army and force them to withdraw from East Pakistan, thus, leading to a democratic set-up and local governance to take over in a peaceful manner.

General Jagjit Singh Aurora, the eastern Army Commander, was given full responsibility for training the cadres, while the responsibility of running of the Eastern Army was left to his deputy, the legendary General JFR Jacob.

A brigadier was assigned to head each of the ten training camps, which they did admirably. We were churning out quite a handful of motivated fighting 'soldiers' every three months, and the numbers kept growing as the influx of refugees increased.

Led and conceptualised by Khandker, the force that was thus formed was called the 'Kilo Force.'

My guru then told me of an instance when the then Chief of Air Staff, Air Chief Marshal PC Lal solved a teething problem of command and control in quick time.

There were a huge number of demands placed on the IAF by the Army for tackling tasks related to the Kilo Force as well as looking after our own army requirements. Gen Jacob was unhappy with the dual command and control of assets in his area—the Central and the Eastern Air Commands provided the air assets at that time in support of all operations in the Eastern theatre.

This was causing unnecessary confusion and delays and affecting smooth running of operations, Jacob felt. In a meeting with the three chiefs who came to Fort William to see how things were progressing, Jacob and Khandker took Air Chief Marshal PC Lal aside and briefed him on the same.

Jacob then requested the Chief of Air Staff (CAS), 'Can you make my life simpler sir?'

Pronto, orders were issued by the Air Chief and the Advanced HQ at Fort William came into being under Air Commodore Solomon Purushottam.

In fact, PC Lal actually 'neutered' the Command HQs who were to now only give administrative support in terms of provisioning of rations, military hardware, and men as and when required. Similarly, during actual operations starting December 3, Gp Capt Chandan Singh was handed over operational control of the helicopter and transport operations, thus delineating control from Eastern Air Command.

It became as simple as that—the army asked for support to the IAF who were placed within the same HQ, and it was approved there and then!

During the same meeting with the CAS, Khandker also requested the IAF to part with the Mystere aircraft, which was being phased out of service in the IAF for use by the new Bangladeshi Air Force. PC Lal was not in favour of arming the fledging air force with fighters just then.

With one armed Chetak helicopter, one armed Otter, and one Dakota, nine officers and fifty-seven men, the Bangladesh Air Force came into being on 28 Sept 1971. Till today, the BAF celebrates this day as their Air Force Day. This was the day that training commenced in Dimapur under the IAF as the Kilo Flight. After the surrender and the formation of the new country, the Kilo Flight aircraft, riddled with bullets but still fly-worthy, were handed over to the Bangladeshis at Dacca.

The story of the Bangladeshi pilots who were trained on IAF aircraft to fire the first shots at their own soil on the night of 3 December 1971 is an interesting one. We shall have that in the subsequent chapters, narrated directly from the horse's mouth!

THE BIRTH OF AN AIR FORCE

AIR CMDE CHANDRA MOHAN SINGLA

In the last chapter on the formation of Kilo Force and the Kilo Flight, I had mentioned that the Kilo Flight was formed out of three aircraft given by the IAF—Chetak, Otter and Dakota. These soon formed the Kilo Flight which was soon to be the Bangladesh Air Force (BAF). These planes were to be flown by Bangladeshi pilots who had crossed over to our country in August 1971. I decided to speak with Air Commodore Chandra Mohan Singla, 82, who was involved in training of these pilots in 1971.

Almost 50 years later, Singla Sir still remembers the events and anecdotes from this special phase of his career as if they happened yesterday.

Flt Lt CM Singla was posted as an instructor at the 112 Helicopter Unit located at Baghdogra in September of 1971. Besides doing some regular operational flying in support of the units in the area of responsibility, the unit was mainly entrusted with carrying out operational training of the rookie pilots who had just graduated out of the Helicopter Training School (HTS) before they went on to fly in operational units.

The war clouds were hanging low and the unit found itself on standby most of the time to undertake operational missions. Amidst all this excitement, a call was received by the Commanding Officer (CO) of the unit, Squadron Leader Naresh Kumar (Later Air Marshal) to send one Qualified Flying Instructor (QFI) to Tezpur. Flt Lt Singla was chosen to go the very next day. There was no clarity of what the mission was and how much time was Singla required to go for.

'I did not want to go for a desk job especially when war was imminent. I promptly went to the CO's office and told him of my apprehensions. I had been recently posted in and wanted to garner as much of instructional experience as possible—especially on the Chetak on which I had limited experience. All my protests fell on deaf years,' says the veteran.

'Pack your bags for 4 to 5 weeks and be ready to move by a transport aircraft tomorrow morning,' his CO ordered.

Dejected and not sure of where he was headed and what kind of job he would be doing, Singla was ready at the tarmac at 8 the next morning when a Dakota aircraft came to ferry him to Tezpur.

At Tezpur, he was received at the tarmac by the then CO of the 115 HU, Squadron Leader Mehtani and taken to the office of the Air Officer Commanding.

'Have you flown a Chetak alone (single Pilot)?' asked the boss. Without waiting for an answer, the AOC went on in his drawl, 'Mama' Mehtani has a chopper ready for you. Take it to Dimapur. Maintenance aspects will be taken care of there, not to worry on that count. All further questions that you have will be clarified at Dimapur after you reach there. Carry On! And happy landings!' said the AOC signaling the meeting to a close.

Happy that he was still on a flying mission, Singla went about preparing his maps and obtaining the radio frequencies and weather data etc. Soon, he was airborne for Dimapur in Nagaland which was just 130 km South East of Tezpur as the crow flies. 'On reaching the air base, I was received by a rickety old jeep on the tarmac. Throwing my luggage at the back, I sat down next to the driver. But the jeep refused to start!' Cursing under his breath, hungry, tired and sweaty after a long day, Singla started his first day at Dimapur pushing the jeep and was soon shown to his ramshackle quarters in a room located in a dilapidated ATC (Air Traffic Control) building very close to where his aircraft was parked.

Dimapur was a small unit commanded by a Flight Lieutenant with fifteen men. Their role was to provide support to the air maintenance (supply drop missions) being carried out by the Dakota to provide the much-needed rations and wherewithal to the troops deployed in the forward areas of Nagaland.

'Living conditions were just about adequate. I have no complaints about the spicy and oily food and the remnants of a mattress on a rickety old bed that was provided!' jokes the veteran.

Things became clearer after Group Captain Chandan Singh, the Station Commander of Jorhat landed at Dimapur in a Dakota the next day. 'I remember it was 28 September, 1971. It had been two days since I had received orders to move,' says Singla Sir.

Chandan Singh briefed the young QFI, 'You are to train three Bangladeshi pilots to fly this Chetak helicopter. Your task begins now. I want them to be fully operational as soon as possible. You will receive all the maintenance support to keep the helicopter flying.'

The Bangla aircrew arrived the same day. 'I had three pupils to train—Squadron Leader Sultan Ahmed and Flight Lieutenant Badrul Alam were ex-PAF pilots whilst Captain Shahabuddin Ahmed used to fly for Pakistan International Airlines.'

'Training soon commenced in full earnest. Ground

training began on the 28 of September itself. 'Little did I know that this date would be nominated as the raising day of the BAF in a few months' time,' quips the veteran.

There was never a moment of respite. Flying continued into the night and the pilots went through many phases of training both on ground and in the air to learn how to handle the machine. The Bangla pilots had flown the fixed wing aircrafts till this time and they had to unlearn some of the practices learnt over time flying the 'normal aircraft.' The helicopter was different, its speed could be dropped to zero, it could move sideways and backwards and the most difficult part was to learn how to hover!

Discarding their fixed wing habits was a problem at first but after sufficient practice, they were fairly comfortable with the hover and other nuances peculiar to the helicopter.

'The pilots were not used to reducing their speeds to almost zero while landing. The very concept of flying itself had to undergo a change,' Singla Sir says. 'Also, their age, matured fixed wing flying habits, distressed state of mind and barely acceptable living conditions made teaching and training a formidable task,' he adds.

Very soon, Singla reported to Chandan Singh that the training was well underway and the pilots were now ready to take on some operational tasks.

Singla Sir describes an event when he had a brush with death during the night navigation training. One day Chandan Singh ordered, 'For the night navigation phase, I want to see your helicopter over Johrat ATC at midnight.' The sky was obscured with clouds and there was possibility of rain. Halfway through the navigation in the pitch darkness, the aircraft encountered intense clouding and had to descend.

The Chetak helicopter was just about good enough for good weather flying.

'Flying on instruments that night, I kept descending inadvertently to avoid the clouds and the rain which had started to pelt down in torrents. We could barely see what was ahead and there was no visual reference. Suddenly, we found ourselves almost brushing the tree tops and were about to shave the tops of some with our rotors! That would have been a doom for us. I pulled up to a decent height and decided that enough was enough. We set course back for Dimapur and landed back safely by the grace of god!'

Although Chandan Sir gave them a mouthful for not reaching Jorhat, they were happy to be alive to fly another day.

THE ARMED CHETAK

It was 8 October, the Indian Air Force Day. Singla was summoned to Jorhat to receive another machine being brought there in a transport aircraft. 'The serial number of the machine as recorded in my flying log book is

Z-364,' says the veteran.

Z-364 was modified by our technicians with two rocket pods—each carrying seven rockets—and was fitted on either side of the aircraft. These pods were taken from the Mystere aircraft which was going out of service at that time. The rockets could be fired in salvo (all together) or in pairs as the situation warranted.

Also fitted inside the compartment behind the pilots was a twin barrel machine gun taken out of another fighter aircraft. The left door of the helicopter had to be removed as the gun barrel protruded out of the helicopter.

The gun firing was done by an operator who sat behind the weapon and swiveled it to aim at the targets. It was just a basic modification and more of a *jugaad*, something that had never been done on any other machine on the IAF inventory. The helicopter flew low and slow and was an easy target for the trigger-happy troops on the ground. Only time would tell if this modification was worth the trouble.

With the extra weight and the additional drag, the aircraft behaved sluggishly. But that was to be expected. 'Chandan Singh and I flew the aircraft to Dimapur as soon as it was assembled at Jorhat. We now had two Chetaks available—one passenger version and one armed.'

They soon had the specialist armament tradesmen and the rockets flown in. What was left was to train the men to fire from the aircraft. 'I was to train the pilots to fire from the aircraft by day and night,' says the ace. 'But then, I too had no experience or clue about firing from a helicopter.' Singla voiced his concern to Chandan Singh, 'We need to harmonize the sights, work out flying parameters and devise tactics and then carry out some target practice. I have no experience in all this—who will guide me?' Singla asked Chandan.

In his characteristic style, Chandan waved away Singla's apprehensions. 'You will learn! I am confident that you will accomplish this task!' Singla remembers with nostalgia, 'This was the first of the many pioneering tasks that I was entrusted with during my long innings in the IAF.'

A simple sight was fitted on the Chetak for aiming and practice began in all earnest. 'After having gotten a hang of the sluggish aircraft, one had to practice aiming and dummy firing at targets. A Dakota was tasked to drop some parachutes over the jungle on the hill slopes on which we wanted to practice actual firing. Unfortunately, these parachutes went right through the canopy of trees of the jungle and could not be sighted from the air—making it impossible to practice target shooting.'

So, it was decided that a parachute would be tied to the ground which would serve as a target. But who was to tie it? The pilots for sure could not leave their machine. Men were taken aboard the helicopter with the parachutes and it hovered over the grassy slopes of the mountain.

The men with the equipment jumped down and began their work. The parachute was stretched over the ground and secured by nailing it to the ground thereby making an excellent target, visible from miles. Singla remembers how he enjoyed learning and teaching his students how to use the helicopter as a weapon delivery platform. 'I found myself enjoying the game— free of rules, regulations and red tape.'

For firing, the helicopter was to climb to a certain height and then dive towards the target. At the correct height and distance from the target, the trigger was pressed and the rockets were on their way.

It was a matter of time that the pupils became accurate in their shooting, and soon the parachute was shredded to bits. 'We had to re-lay another target and continue our practice till such time I could report to the boss at Jorhat that the three pupils could deliver the weapons reasonably by day.'

Chandan Singh now asked the foreign pilots to design an emblem for the helicopter and also give it a name and number. After a lot of lively deliberations and excitement amongst them, they came up with the answer. A red roundel with the East Pakistan map superimposed on it was to be painted on the tail stabilizer of the helicopter. The helicopter was to be registered as 'EBR' which stood for 'East Bangladesh Rifles' actually. Singla sir narrates, 'Overnight, the Chetak with new markings was rechristened and thereafter, flew on the call sign 'Echo-Bravo-Romeo'.

Singla Sir concludes, 'By all accounts, this was the first aircraft of the Bangladesh Air Force. My log book entries of flying the aircraft change from Z-364 to EBR from October onwards.'

Very soon, in early October, Singla Sir was back at his unit in Baghdogra having completed his task at Dimapur. It had been time well spent and with a lot of takeaways for the QFI. 'I now found life boring with routine flying activities and no excitement!' he says.

But this period of so-called 'boredom' was short lived. He was soon summoned—this time by name, at Dimapur to carry out further training and ended up flying in the war from there itself.

KILO FLIGHT AND THE WAR

War seemed to be imminent. There was tension everywhere while they continued their training, this time by night. The mission was to train the pupils to fire the weapons by night. Singla just had a month to accomplish this task and flying by night was gradually stepped up, first in moonlit conditions and thereafter graduating to pitch dark conditions.

The Chetak, by the way, has not been cleared to fly in pitch dark conditions even today.

With the limited and unreliable instrumentation available for flying the aircraft by night, this was no mean task. 'Nevertheless, we fired on targets by night and gained adequate proficiency to call ourselves "Fully Operational" (Fully Ops) by day and night,' says Singla.

It was December. Singla got summons to go and meet Group Captain Chandan Singh on 1 December at Jorhat.

'He told me that a strike was to be launched into East Pakistan within a few days from an unmanned airfield near Agartala.'

Chandan Singh asked him, 'Can your boys navigate, strike the target accurately and return to base?' Smiling, Singla replied, 'We are all good to go sir but about returning, I cannot say!'

In the pitch darkness, navigating back after a tension filled mission was what worried Singla. After discussions with the Station Commander, it was decided that the landing areas would be lit up by one 'petromax' lamp which would be covered with a perforated tin. This was the best that could be done in the prevailing circumstances, anyway. The first strike into East Pakistan was on!

2 December, 1971

Singla and his pilots flew to Kailashaher, an abandoned airfield near Tripura just on the eastern border with East Pakistan. The strike was to be launched from a small airstrip at Teliamura. Group Captain Chandan Singh was there too, overseeing the preparations and pumping the morale of the boys.

Squadron Leader Sultan and Flight Lieutenant Alam were detailed for the first mission on the night of 3 December, the day Pakistan declared hostilities on the western front. The aircraft was loaded with 14 rockets meant to be delivered on the fuel storage tanks at Narayanganj just 30 odd kilometers south of Dacca.

Singla supervised their start-up and wished them luck with their firing and safe return. 'The checks and procedures were well imbibed into their system, I realised, as they took off. The pilots had forgotten to switch off their navigation lights and were clearly visible from miles!' In normal day to day routine operations, the navigation lights are meant to be put on and flown. This, however, can prove fatal during war since the enemy would be able to spot the aircraft from miles. Singla got onto the radio set and gave them a call to switch them off.

The helicopter immediately melted into the darkness and was on its way to fire the first shots in the war against Pakistan in the east.

Similarly, there was an armed Otter which took off from yet another base with similar armament to be delivered on East Pakistani soil. This was also flown by the Pakistani pilots but that story I shall keep for later.

Singla says, 'The Pakistanis never expected such an audacious attack by a helicopter and transport aircraft and were completely taken by surprise. The armament

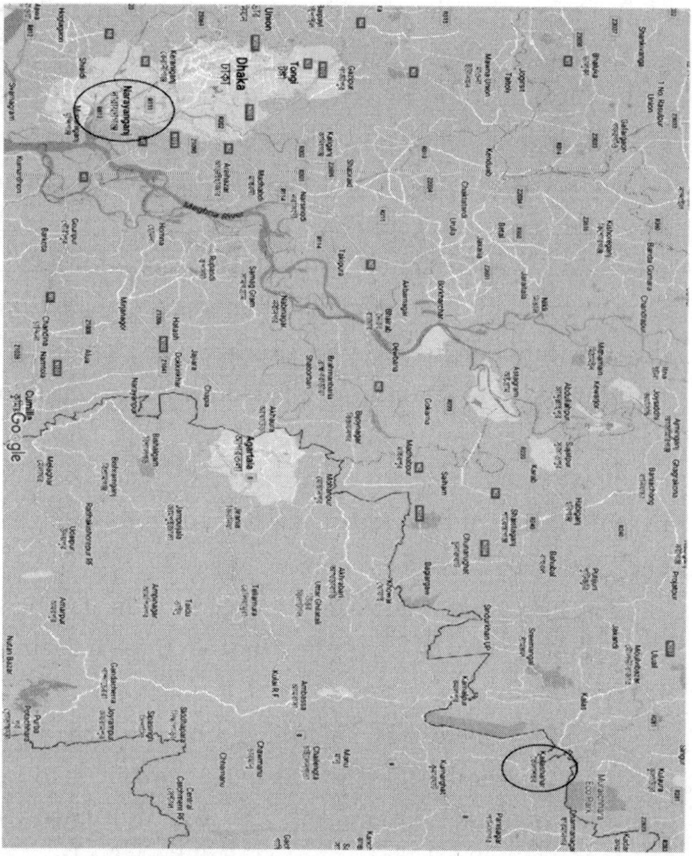

From Kailashaher to Narayanganj—the first shots fired.

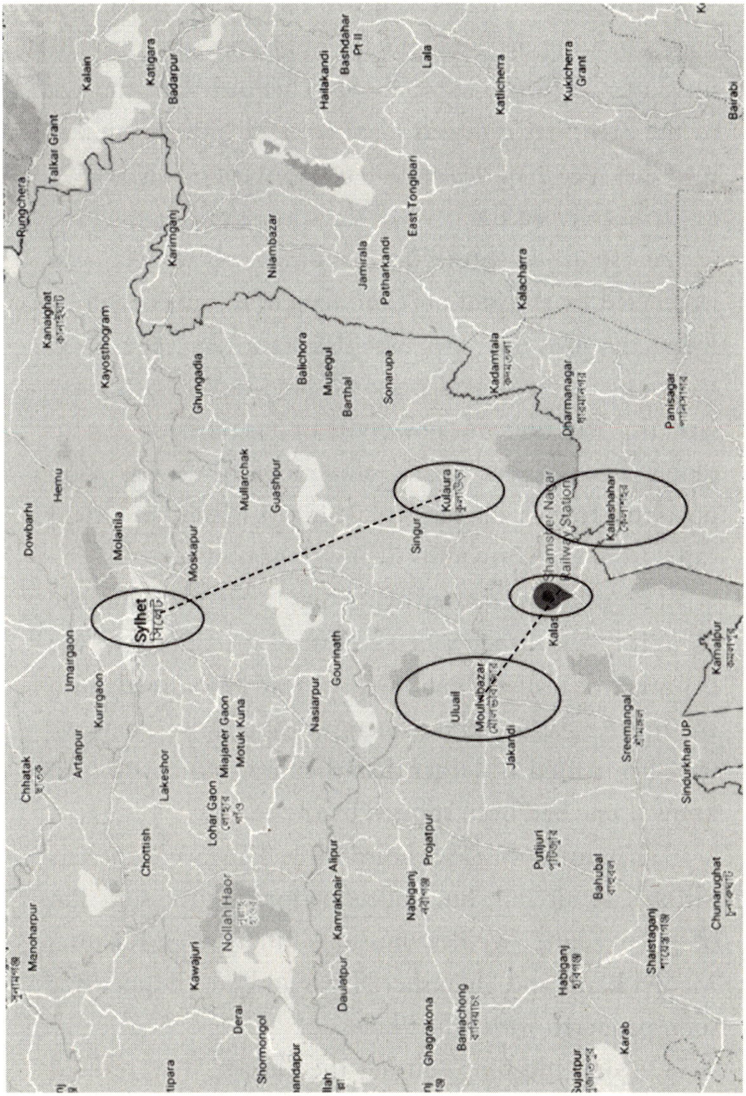

Shamsher Nagar-Maulvi Bazar axis as well as the Kalaura-Sylhet axis.

was delivered on target and the fuel dump burst into flames lighting up the night sky of Dacca's suburbs. The mission was recovered safely at a helipad with the use of the petromax lights as planned, and Indira Gandhi's recorded speech of declaration of war went on air as soon as Delhi received the news of the success of the mission.'

As soon as hostilities commenced, Singla was instructed by thc Station Commander to take charge of flying the missions into East Pakistan. 'We were given Pakistani currency and personal Sten-carbines to carry with us.' The unit was now more or less established with tentage, manpower, spares and mobility. It was soon operating from Kailashaher. Living was in tents and food came from the army units deployed nearby.

The missions started with Singla Sir manning the cockpit in the armed Chetak most of the time. 'On the first night, I realised that only when we flew directly into the muzzle flashes of the enemy weapons, we knew we were being fired at. Other than that, it was impossible to know if one had been spotted by the enemy.'

'The muted thuds we heard while flying were not bats hitting our aircraft, but bullets perforating the soft skin of our machine. We flew missions to targets in Kalaura, Maulvi Bazar and Shamsher Nagar and the chopper was soon peppered with bullet holes.'

On one morning, during the checks, they realised that although the bullets had gone through the thin skin of the aircraft, no major component had suffered any damage. 'The helicopter did not have any armour plating as the latest ones do and luck was on our side, the machine remained fly-worthy.' It was decided to paint the bullet holes and number them so that one could find newer ones after every mission. 'After a while, this exercise was given up. There were far too many holes to count and number!' says Singla Sir.

Flight Lieutenant Ramakrishna was the dynamic engineering officer who saw to it that the aircraft was available for missions. He and his men had their hands full to keep the two Chetaks ready at all times since the missions were coming thick and fast. The helicopter kept coming back with more holes and thorough checks had to be carried out after each sortie. Ramakrishna and his bunch of technicians kept patching up the holes and checking for internal damage as the helicopters kept flying.

Singla remembers with a smile, 'After the patch repairs, one day, I asked Rama if the bird was serviceable. He countered my question with, "Will you fly her?" When I replied in the affirmative, he was quick to answer, "Then she is serviceable!" The Chetak had earned so much name for itself that the army personnel from the neighbouring units came to look at the flying sieve!'

'In the first few sorties, I handed over my wallet and watch to Rama...just in case....But later, I became more confident of returning and carried them on myself on missions!' Rama also made life easier for the crew by modifying a weapon carrying hook at the back of the seats where their personal weapons could be carried safely.

Singla has vivid memories of flying missions during the war and he describes some interesting ones to me.

Having flown three missions on the night of 6 December and taking a lot of hits, they flew seven missions on 7 December too.

'We were initially given fighter aircraft cover to ensure that the ground troops kept their heads down while we attacked the targets, but this was discontinued because, firstly, the small silhouette of the helicopter was not visible to the fighter, especially when viewed from above, as it merged with the green background and secondly, after the initial few days, the IAF had achieved almost total air superiority over the East Pakistani airspace, and the only threat we had was from ground based anti-aircraft guns.'

Flying from Kailashahar, they engaged targets in Darbart, Brahmanbaria, Daudkandi and Narsingdi Road and many more.

On the night of 7 December, Singla was given a target of Pakistani troops crossing en masse over a river near Kalaura. 'The river was teeming with boats of all sizes and we decided to take on the largest of them. I hit the boat with a salvo of two rockets and then realised that the boat was carrying innocent civilians!'

The attack was abandoned and the matter reported

to the higher-ups. 'Till today, I regret targeting innocent civilians, albeit by mistake,' says the veteran pilot.

IV Corps of our army was pushing westwards and intense battles were taking place on the Shamsher Nagar-Maulvi Bazar axis as well as the Kalaura-Sylhet axis. While carrying out missions in support of our ground troops, the helicopter took one too many hits and Rama reported to Singla that the damage was now severe and the helicopter needed to be grounded.

'But if you are willing, I shall make her ready,' he added. In the heat of the battle, and to ensure that we continued to put the enemy down, a decision was taken. We decided to fly her after some mandatory checks and a few repairs. 'We did a couple of sorties to Shamsher Nagar that night in the bullet riddled aircraft,' he tells me.

The heliborne missions were also underway now with our Mi-4s ferrying across the Gorkha troops across the Meghna River, which I shall narrate shortly. The armed Chetak was used to give covering fire during these missions.

One day, the light was fading and it was decided not to send in the Chetak since there was fear of fratricide—with opposing troops in close proximity of each other, they could end up shooting at our own troops. Therefore, the Mi4 missions were called off for the night.

The Gorkha officer doing the liaising desperately wanted the missions to continue and he argued with

Chandan Singh on ground. Chandan Singh explained to him in his calm tone that any more attempts at the Special Heliborne Operations (SHBO) would prove to be fatal and this would be continued in the morning the next day.

But the keen Gurkha was not able to understand the logic and continued to pester Chandan Singh.

Exasperated, Chandan Singh, in his booming voice, said, 'SHBO missions will not happen now! Go on! Shoot me if you wish with your pistol!'

Along with grit and passion, one also needs a calm and cool mind to lead in times of war. I recount another such moment which proves this observation.

'One day Chandan Singh and I went to Sylhet airfield to ascertain if it was free of the Pakis. As we came in to land and were just a few feet off the ground, a machine gun opened up from a bunker next to the runway and surprised us. Thankfully, the gunner wasn't accurate, otherwise, I wouldn't be here to tell you the story!' says Singla laughing.

Flying away from the danger, Singla asked Chandan, 'Sir, we can go back and give him a load of our rockets, they will silence him forever!' Chandan was not interested and he asked to be flown back to base. It was so good to have a commander like Chandan who had a solid head on his shoulders and at the same time, was dynamic and bold.

On the way back, they landed on a riverbed where they saw some fishing activity. Using their Pakistani currency, they picked up some fresh fish which made for a feast that night.

On 16 December, Singla flew to Dacca for the surrender ceremony along with his co-pilot Squadron Leader Chaudhary. On the potholed tarmac lay a lot of abandoned equipment of the Pakistani army. Singla managed to get himself a belt of Sabre aircraft cannon shells. Later, this booty was shared between all the pilots at Agartala. 'I still have my piece of victory with me,' Singla Sir tells me with glee!

On 18 December, Singla was ordered to take the bullet-ridden Chetak to Dacca and hand it over to the new country. The other Chetak followed to get Singla back.

It was an emotional moment when he shook hands with the three brave Bangladeshi pilots—Sultan, Badrul Alam, and Shahabuddin Ahmed on the tarmac.

They stayed at the BAF Officers Mess that night and celebrated their victory. 'Shahabuddin wrote his address in Dacca on a Pakistani currency note and handed it to me as a souvenir. I still have it with me!' Singla remarks wistfully.

The Bangladeshi pilots kept the sten machine carbines issued to them as their booty of the war. Next morning, the three of them saw the second Chetak off at the tarmac. A crate of scotch had been kept in the passenger compartment as a gift from them.

For his stellar role in the war, Squadron Leader CM Singla was awarded the Vir Chakra. On the other side, Sultan, his co-pilot for the missions he flew for the independence of his country was awarded the 'Bir Uttam'.

'We formed a unique crew—decorated for bravery by two nations,' says Singla as we sign off.

MUDDY RUNWAYS

AIR CMDE AD KARANDIKAR

I had run into Air Commodore AD Karandikar (Kandy Sir) many times during my career in the IAF. I knew him as the VIP pilot who only flew the Prime Minister, the President and other such VIPs. He was one of the first IAF pilots to be trained to fly the Boeing 737. For us helicopter boys, VIP trips meant picking up the VIP from the airport and transporting him to some remote helipad and getting him back to the airport—only to be taken away in the mighty jet flown by Kandy Sir. These were short and sweet trips where we hardly got time to see or interact with the VIPs. We always looked up in awe at the Communication Squadron pilots who flew for long hours with these important people and got themselves photographed too!

At that time, I did not know that the Boeing pilot I had interacted with had been baptized by fire in the 1971 war.

Furthermore, little did I know then that I would be interviewing him one day to find out about his exploits as a flying officer in 1971—flying the most intriguing aircraft—the Dakota, in the most remarkable and trying circumstances.

'It was 7 December, I was called by Gp Capt Chandan Singh, the Station Commander to do a trip to Kumbhigram (Silchar) in the Dakota.'

'And what he said thereafter floored me. He asked me, "Are you confident of flying the Dak alone?"'

Without waiting for an answer from the bewildered Karandikar, the Commander in his quintessential way, told him, 'Carry on! And safe flying!'

The Dakota was a transport plane meant to be flown by two pilots and two more crew members. The cockpit was large enough and some of the switches and controls were accessible to the co-pilot only. Karandikar sat down to think how he would accomplish the duties of the entire crew in the cockpit without endangering the aircraft and its occupants. It was a tough ask and his thoughts took him back to his training days.

Karandikar had been posted to 43 Squadron in the January of 1971 to fly the Dakota aircraft. The 'Dak', as it is known, had already been in service for a long time in the IAF. The aircraft had been modified for military use from the original DC-3 variant and could fly at about 250 km per hour and go about 2,500 km on a full tank. The aircraft had done yeoman service in the Second World War and continues to be in service even today. Very recently, on the occasion of the 72nd Republic Day of our country, it performed a fly-past at Rajpath and also endeared the audience in the recently concluded 'Aero-India' at the Yelahanka Air Force Base.

'I had already spent a few years in the IAF, being commissioned in 1967 and had adequate experience on the An-12 which was the workhorse of the IAF at that time,' Kandy Sir started.

Flying the Dak was new to him and he had to get operational on the aircraft by flying 100 hours in the NEFA, 'North East Frontier Agency' as the north-eastern states were known then. 'I was called the "Keen Kumar" of the squadron since I always volunteered for trips and was always ready to take to the skies. Gaining the 100 hours wasn't easy. One barely got 15 to 20 minutes of Captain Flying[1] whilst on the supply drop missions,' he claims. But with perseverance, his log book soon had the required flying hours and within a few months, he was

---

1 Captain of the aircraft is responsible for the safety of the aircraft and its crew and passengers. He is assisted by the co-pilot. To become a captain, one has to fly in the captain seat along with a flying instructor who can handle the aircraft from the co-pilots seat.

declared an Instrument Rated Captain[2] on the Dakota.

The genocide in Pakistan was all over the news at that time. The eastern region was flooded with a mass of population exodus from East Pakistan. The entire eastern command was soon declared a disturbed zone under Operation Cactus Lily. 'For us "piddly" flying officers, it meant that rations would be free and there would be no fat mess bills. It also meant that we would not get any dearness allowance!' says the veteran with a smile.

'Bunkers were being dug up and camouflage painting done on all roofs. There was a flurry of construction activity all around which signaled to us that something big was in the offing,' remembers Kandy Sir.

'In early May, I, along with Flying Officer KS Rajan, Flight Lieutenant PC Chopra (Navigator) and Flight Lieutenant Biswas (Flt Signaller) were selected by our Commanding Officer, Wing Commander KC 'Koka' Sharma for a detachment to fly for Eastern Command for about fifteen days. We airlifted bridging and other equipment, army personnel wearing *lungis* (Simple wraparounds worn by local village folk) to generally unused landing grounds like Ambari, Cooch Bihar, Balurghat on the border, and also to Agartala. We were told to keep quiet about what we did or saw. These places

2 Instrument rating is given to captain of the aircraft as per his flying experience and proficiency. With a higher rating, he is allowed to fly in poorer conditions of visibility and clouds as compared to a lower rated pilot.

were also in proximity to the training camps where the Indian Army was training the Mukti Bahini.'

This entailed a lot of flying in the notorious pre-monsoon weather of that region. There were a few days when they flew with only lychees as sustenance during the entire day, resulting in achingly sour teeth and a rumbling stomach by the evening. During those flights, Kandy Sir was fortunate to meet Brig Shahbeg Singh, the mercurial Commander of the Counter Insurgency School at Vairangte and Col MAG Osmani of the Mukti Bahini.

The pilots of the squadron were soon sent to Agra to get trained on flying para-jump missions—a very important requirement for the impending war.

And how did they land at these short and unused landing strips? Well, that is another interesting story!

These landing strips were just short kutcha runways which were unmarked. There was no Air Traffic Control and almost no one on ground to ensure that things were safe to land. Also, the flat grassy runway surface offered a good grazing ground for the cattle which invariably blocked the runway. 'We came in at low level and then descended in a circuit pattern over the disused runway. Thereafter, it was mandated to do a couple of runs along the runway at very low levels to scare away the cattle, after which we did a short circling approach to land,' says the ace.

'There was just about adequate length to stop the aircraft on these short landing strips, and often, we landed in tail winds since only one direction was available for takeoff and landing. One had to literally sit on brakes and stop the heavily loaded aircraft, and if the conditions were wet, there were chances of skidding on the muddy surface of the runway,' remembers Karandikar. 'Take-offs were trickier, since the big bird would climb very slowly, just skimming the tree tops.'

'The cattle soon were trained, they moved away as soon as we were overhead and were back grazing after we landed!' exclaims the transport pilot.

'I knew nothing about Kilo Flight till I was detailed to join them on 1 December 1971, along with Squadron Leader SK Chaudhary, a senior pilot and QFI (Qualified Flying Instructor), flying in to Dimapur where they were based. The *raison de etre* of creating this unit was essentially to give these pilots a sense of participation in the war to liberate East Pakistan from the Pakistani rulers,' says Karandikar.

The aircraft Kandy Sir was allotted was HJ-882. It had nosed over the previous day during a full power run by a technician and both propeller tips had gotten bent! The aircraft was declared serviceable after the propellers were changed and a caution was given not to use maximum RPM. 'HJ-882 was like my personal possession till 16 December,' says the veteran.

He goes on, 'As I remember, there were 9 PAF pilots, the senior-most being Squadron Leader Sultan Mahmud (who later became the Chief of the Bangladesh Air Force) who was a helicopter pilot. I remember a Flight Lieutenant Alam who had flown F-86 fighter, another Flight Lieutenant Alam who was a C-130 pilot, a Capt Shahbuddin from a regional airline and one Sharafuddin. Sultan Mahmud and the fighter pilot, Badrul Alam were trained on an Alouette (Chetak) helicopter by Squadron Leader CM Singla, the rest on Otter aircraft by Squadron Leader Ghoshal. Both aircraft were fitted with 30 mm rocket pods and a machine gun firing sideways in the rear, the door being removed on the left side, operated by an airman crew.'

There had been talk of equipping a Dakota in a similar fashion, but it was never done. Probably, it would have taken a long time for the available pilots to build up the necessary skill levels. Also, none of the Bangladeshi pilots under the Kilo Flight banner were trained to fly a Dakota at that time.

However, during the earlier part of the year, two Bangladeshis were trained at Dimapur on a civil registered Dakota which was handed over to Bangladesh for use in their airline—the Bangla Biman. The same crashed in Feb 1972 killing Captain Shaqeel and four others. Shaqeel had been trained by Squadron Leader SK Chaudhary who was flying with Karandikar as part of the Kilo Force.

The ex-PAF guys used to tell us tales of the unique privileges enjoyed by military officers in Pakistan. Apart from unbelievable salaries, unique privileges like duty-free import of whatever they wanted was the cause of some envy! Due to such privileges, they enjoyed the attention of celebrities and film stars and were often treated like them!

I remember on a visit to Chittagong after the war, I was talking to an old Mess orderly like we usually do, enquiring about his well-being. As soon as I asked him, the man burst into tears. He told me that no officer had ever spoken to him except for ordering him around.

THE LOOMING WAR

'AN 12s were not used in the Eastern theatre but Caribou aircraft were used to drop a few bombs over Tezgaon airfield on one or two occasions,' Karandikar remembers. This was done at night after complete air superiority had been achieved.

AN12s were used with very good results in the western theatre for the Changa Manga forests, the SUI Gas plants and to bomb Skardu airfield. Wing Commander VB Vasisht, the CO was awarded a MVC and the Flight Commander Squadron Leader Ahluwalia a VrC. One Navigator, Squadron Leader PB Kalra also got a VrC.

'The monsoons came and went and so did the festival of Diwali and we kept waiting for the balloon to go up. Aggressive postures were being taken on both sides and little skirmishes kept the situation hot.'

'On 2 December 1971, we moved bag and baggage to Kailashaher, a small airstrip with almost no infrastructure. Having landed there after the usual low-level run, we were met by the Air Observation Post Pilots of the Indian Army who flew the vintage Auster aircraft and were tasked to direct artillery fire on to the enemy as our own forces advanced.'

'The space on the tarmac to manoeuvre the aircraft was minimal and the space available for us to live even worse! As per the pecking order, I, being the junior most, got to live in the passenger hall of the terminal building where a few rooms were occupied by the seniors. After rolling out my bed on the floor, I got some sleep and every morning, I became accustomed to load up my little household into my Dakota not knowing where I would be by the end of the day.'

'I practically lived in my flying overalls and food was basic and simple. Our only cook produced dal, roti, and a vegetable from whatever was available locally and we all ate the hot food happily, without cribbing. Later, well into the war, when the Chetak helicopter operated from our base, it would land in enemy territory and get us some good fish and other stuff to spice up our lives!'

In the evenings when there was some breathing time, the pilots and other crew sat down together and listened to the radio to understand the larger picture. Some of them had seen the Indo-Pak war of 1965 and had stories to tell from that time too.

'From the '65 experience, we would often conjecture where all this fighting would lead to and what would be the endgame; as the war progressed and the situation became clearer, we were now sure that East Pakistan would soon be a separate nation. It was just a matter of time before we had a brand-new neighbour.'

'The balloon finally went up on 3 December and we were quite excited to be the soldiers fighting for our nation. The first attack into Bangladesh was done by the Chetak aircraft piloted by Sultan Mahmud and Alam who attacked the oil storage tanks at Chittagong and set it aflame. Simultaneously, the Otter aircraft piloted by the other Alam and Sharafuddin went and attacked the fuel depot at Narayanganj and scored hits too.'

Group Captain Chandan Singh showed remarkable leadership qualities when he tasked the all, "Bangla" crew who were new to these aircraft to fire the first shots to win them their freedom. Later on, the senior and more experienced Indian crew flew in these machines alongside the Bangla pilots on subsequent missions.

Karandikar had an interesting fact to narrate about the Otter mission. 'Originally, Chandan Singh had briefed the Otter Pilots to attack the Petrol Oil and Lubricants (POL) dump at Dacca. As the Otter was starting up for the sortie, Chandan Sir realised that it would be too risky to send the aircraft to a heavily defended Dacca and so changed the target to Narayanganj. And do you know who went running to the aircraft to give this message? It was me!'

'May be, the lives of the Otter pilots were saved that day due to this timely decision.'

'From what I remember, both the aircrafts got lost coming back in the pitch-dark night. Luckily, we had ATC controllers at Teliamura where the Chetak was recovered while the Otter landed at Kumbhigram just with a few litres of fuel remaining!'

In the wee hours of the morning, Kandy sir flew his Dakota to Kumbhigram with essential oils and the ground crew to recover the plane to the fight from Kailashaher.

The task for Kandy Sir's Dak was to undertake sorties on an as required basis between Kailashahar, Kumbhigram and Dimapur. 'I also flew one troop insertion sortie into enemy territory at Shamshernagar on 5 December. The Air Observation Post (AOP) pilots flying in the area reported heavy Pakistani shelling on that landing ground and that prevented any further missions by the Dakota.'

'We flew all missions in the first part of the war at low levels—that is, at 300 to 500 feet above ground. These sorties were, no doubt stressful since the pilots and crew had to look out for birds, obstructions as well as enemy gunfire. Later on, once the Pakistani Air Force was decimated in the east, we flew at 5,000 feet, which was less bothersome to say the least! We were clear of enemy ground fire and navigation was also easy,' Kandy sir admits.

The Dak carried all logistic support to keep the Kilo Flight aircraft fly worthy as well as brought in the POL, rockets and ammunition for the guns. Karandikar also flew a few 'propaganda' missions which involved dropping of leaflets over the enemy territory.

WITH THE CHOPPER GUYS

The helicopters joined in around 5 December in the evening. Along with General Sagat Singh, Group Captain Chandan Singh had planned to use helicopters for insertion of troops into East Pakistan. The airlift of 4/5 Gurkhas across the Meghna River started the race of Indian commanders towards Dacca.

'It was fun to interact with the Chopper Boys, but finding a place to sleep further became a problem! We were packed like sardines in the passenger hall of the airfield now. There were some immediate seniors and juniors in the crowd. It was good to meet some of them after our association at the academy. We shared news of what we learnt on missions and on the radio. We came to know of a few of our friends who had lost their lives in the operations but there was no time to grieve. We chatted through the night till sleep overtook us.'

'The chopper boys did an excellent job without a single casualty although they got a few bullets into their machines. Their *josh* and morale was sky high—evident when every single and some double hands were raised when the Flight commander asked for volunteers!' says Kandy sir.

Later the operations shifted southwards from Sylhet and other troops of 57 Mountain Division were inserted without mishap, touchwood, by the Mi-4's of three units, namely 111 HU, 115 HU and 110 HU.

'As the operations progressed, a large number of casualties started landing up in their return trips as well as by road. Most of them were apparently mine-blast injuries and the lower half of the bodies sustained maximum damage. It wasn't a pleasant sight at all. The soldiers arriving had their oozing wounds barely covered with some gauze. While some of the soldiers were in coma, some were delirious and required to be sedated.'

Our men had suffered so much pain for the independence of other people in a foreign land.

The doctors had a makeshift medical assistance room where the preliminary stabilisation of patients was done before they were boarded into the waiting Dakota and Packet aircraft to be taken to various hospitals right up to Calcutta.

'One thing that was remarkable about these doctors was that they worked day and night without rest and did not discriminate between the patients. Be it an injured POW or an Indian Jawan, the priority for airlift was given as per the grievousness of the injury,' says the Air Commodore with pride. 'Since the Dak wasn't modified to carry patients, we would keep the stretchers on the floor or make the casualties sit, if they could, on the canvas seats in our aircraft. We also had to ensure smooth rides for them since there was no way to secure the stretchers. The smell of blood coupled with the smell of ammonia and medicines still makes me shudder,' remembers Karandikar.

Meanwhile the end of the war was certain and East Pakistan was capitulating. It was 15 December. The 4/5 GR troops who had fought the battle of Sylhet and won hands down had to be airlifted to Agartala. They had fought well and deserved to be back to their barracks as soon as possible to recuperate. Young Karandikar was detailed to fly these troops back home in his trustworthy Dak.

'I flew through the day and into the night almost up to midnight carrying out 15 take-offs and landings between Kailashaher and Agartala. It was back-breaking work, but the happiness we saw on the returning soldier's faces was tonic for us to go on! I remember that the take-offs and landings from both these airfields was not easy especially at night.' Kailashaher had just six sets of 'goosenecks' (thick burning wicks dipped in oil) placed at the beginning of the runway.

'Agartala was the worst. It had just a few lights placed on only one edge of the runway! Aligning the aircraft to the runway was a problem and so was depth perception. This coupled with the short length of the strips meant that there was no margin for error. Every time I was aligned for landing at Agartala, I would reconfirm from the ATC as to which side of the runway the lights were placed!'

'Having been in the field of military aviation for so many years myself, I can say with absolute certainty that the pilots of those days were a class apart. To fly such big machines which had just the bare instruments and no worthwhile "auto pilot" to help you fly, especially at night, and that too land on an unlighted runway needed guts and above all, perfect flying skills that the new generation of "button pilots" don't have! It was pure "seat of the pants" flying, relying on your guts and excellent training, of course. Ask any pilot of today if he would do what those guys did in 1971, and you will get a big "no" for an answer for sure!'

The Dakotas moved Kilo Flight, lock, stock and barrel to Agartala around the 9-10 December. 'Their role in the war was now almost negligible and they were excited to get back to their own independent country with the aeroplanes to form the Bangladesh Air Force.'

'Have you seen that famous photo of the surrender at Dacca?' Kandy sir asked.

'I have my little story about that too! On 16 December, I was allowed by Group Captain Chandan

Singh to go to Dacca in the Choppers that were going there for the surrender ceremony. I flew with my friends and was amazed at the reception at Dacca after landing. En route, we had seen the silent anti-aircraft guns of the Pakistanis and the troops lined up next to them with their arms placed on the ground. The jeering crowds at Dacca were lifting us as heroes and carrying us on their shoulders. There was a happy mayhem on the streets which I remember clearly.

I was standing right next to the table when the document was being signed, however, I saw some of my army course-mates at the venue and went to meet and greet them. If I hadn't, I would have also been there in that historic photograph!' says the veteran pilot.

'The war had ended, and ended happily for us.' Kandy Sir goes on, 'I had flown a total of forty-nine sorties—of which five were as single pilot on the Dakota— in fourteen days, including fifteen on one day! It had been an experience of a lifetime for me. Although I did not face many enemy bullets due to the kind of flying that the Dakota did, it was a great experience to land on unprepared short runways and that too, at night, without lights and of course, sometimes all alone in the cockpit—something that I never got to do in the rest of my long innings in the IAF. That was indeed baptism by fire for a fledging pilot like me!'

We had begun this conversation talking about flying

the Dak with just Kandy Sir in the cockpit (single pilot) and while navigating through the stories of the war, we had almost forgotten this interesting aspect.

'Sir! We haven't spoken about your experience of flying all alone so far!' I exclaim to him as we wind up the chat.

'Oh yes! We have spoken of everything else except that…' he replied and carried on. 'I indeed was in a bit of a trauma as to how I will handle the aircraft all alone when it had been designed to be flown by two and more. I decided to fly it from the left seat that I was most comfortable from (the left seat was the captain seat). The levers that operated the undercarriage and flaps were on the side of the co-pilot. Also, I had to do all the checks myself without the help of the second mate in the cockpit to monitor if all was going well. I realised a thing or two about cockpit crew resource management which was just taught in theory in our training!'

'The real difficult part was the take-off from the short runways. There were trees looming large in front and one had to establish a decent rate of climb to clear them, however, for this, one had to get the undercarriage up as soon as possible to reduce the drag. So, for the single pilot, one had to first unstick clear of the ground, leave the right hand from the throttles which were at maximum, hold the controls steady with the left hand and then bend fully to the right to reach out to the lever to put up the wheels which required some doing.'

'An inadvertent pullback on the stick while doing this would mean that you stalled the aircraft and crashed and if you pushed the controls forward, the trees would get you! And god forbid, if there was an engine failure just then—only "HE" could save you,' says the veteran.

'In flight, it was an eerie feeling in the cockpit and the workload was high, especially at night, with the ethereal glow of the ultra violet lighting flooding the cockpit. Also, at night, the Far East was pretty much blacked out and the moon and the stars were one's only company if the weather gods were happy. All in all, the solo experience did wonders to my confidence on the aircraft and myself—a confidence that carried me through my long innings in the Indian Air Force.'

Air Commodore Arun Dattatreya Karandikar retired from the IAF after 30 years of glorious service in 1997. He holds the record for the most number of hours flown by a military pilot (12,980 Hours) and finds his name in the *Limca Book of Records.*

(A few weeks after this interview, Air Commodore Karandikar passed away due to Covid-19. May his soul rest in peace.)

HELICOPTER OPERATIONS

AIR CMDE RAM MOHAN SRIDHARAN

Air Cmde Ram Mohan Sridharan was born on 6 November 1947 at Kannur in Kerala. His father was one of the first of the paratroopers of the Medical Corps.

Passing out of the National Defence Academy in December 1967, 'Doc' Sridharan as he is popularly known, was commissioned as a helicopter pilot in the IAF in June 1969. He was fully operational on the MI-4 helicopter by the time the war started in December 1971, and flew a large number of missions as part of 110 Helicopter Unit, then based at Kumbhigram (near Silchar in Assam).

He has amassed more than 8,000 hours of flying during his tenure in the IAF where he rose to the rank of an Air Commodore before he retired in 2003. The ace pilot has taken part in operations all across the country including the 'Operation Pawan' in Sri Lanka and 'Operation Meghdoot' in the Siachen. He has held many important posts in the IAF being at the helm of Helicopter and Transport operations. He has also had the distinction of flying many VIPs like Indira Gandhi and Rajiv Gandhi, Narasimha Rao, Sri Lankan President Jayawardane, Pope John Paul and Yasser Arafat, to name a few. He also has been awarded the coveted Vayu Sena Medal for distinguished service by the President of India.

In this story about helicopter operations during the 1971 war, Sridharan narrates the story of how the IAF helicopters played an important role in the liberation of Bangladesh.

The eight helicopters with the different VIPs on board had landed in East Pakistan late in the afternoon for the ceremony and post the historic event, they were going to take off from a brand new country—Bangladesh! Each one of them had played a major role in the liberation and birth of the new country, but this had been achieved at phenomenal human and material costs.

'We were excited and drove from the Tezgaon (Dacca) airport to the Race Course in open jeeps to see history in the making. As we drove out of the airport, we got a glimpse of how parts of the town had been damaged in the war.' However, the historic monuments and important buildings had been spared which spoke so much about the attitude of our Armed Forces even in war.

Gen Jagjit Singh Aurora—the Eastern Army Commander, Air Mshl HS Dewan, the AOC-in-C Eastern Air Command and Vice-Admiral Krishnan, FOC-in-C of the Eastern Naval Command and the most charismatic hero of '71, General Sagat Singh, besides a large number of VIPs and staff of the Command HQs located at Calcutta and Shillong had been airlifted by the eight helicopters to Dacca for the ceremony.

'We were so happy that the war was finally coming to an end and we, being part of such a historic event, made us euphoric,' says the veteran helicopter pilot. 'It was such an exciting time, and as we went to the venue, locals lined up along the path—cheered and shouted themselves hoarse. We had been so much a part of their happiness and we were their heroes,' remembers Doc Sir.

It was getting dark as they headed back from the ceremony. 'The VIPs who had come along with us for the historic signing of the surrender had to get back into India. As we waited for them to come back to the helicopters, Gen Sagat Singh got us pilots into a huddle and told us, "I am so very happy with the performance of the IAF in Operation "Cactus Lily" and "Jackpot". As I had promised you all before the operations began, we shall be celebrating our victory and usher in the new year at the Dacca Intercontinental Hotel on the 31st of

December. I want you to be a part of my "Celebratory Champagne moment" on that day. So be seeing you there!"'

The fall of Dacca had brought a swift end to the war and East Pakistan had capitulated in 13 days, thanks to some audacious offensive operations led by Gen Sagat Singh and his 4 Corps which was addressing the eastern border of East Pakistan. The IAF had a major part to play in this decisive victory since they had carried out the massive troop insertion by helicopters and fixed wing aircraft at places around Dacca so as to put pressure on the Pakistani military to surrender.

OVERALL ARMY PLAN

As per the literature available, the higher directions received from Army HQ to Eastern Army Commander did not make a mention of the capture of Dacca as a Depth Objective[3] at all. It had been decided that three plus divisions located on the western borders of East Pakistan would attack all along the western front so as to threaten the immediate and depth objectives in their line of advance. From the eastern side, it was the 4 Corps led

3 The military objective, as governed by the overall political objective gives out directions to the commanders in the field how the particular campaign or part of the offensive will be fought. Objectives could be primary, intermediate or depth objectives. War will be fought in phases and the depth objective if captured will be in line with the overall aim as defined.

by Gen Sagat Singh which was to move from east to west in the general line of Dacca.

Sagat had other ideas right from the beginning—well before the war had started—he had realised that it would be very difficult to cross the Meghna river which flowed almost north-south and was a natural line of defence of the Dacca Garrison. At that time, the Army did not have the wherewithal of crossing rivers in such large numbers. This is where the IAF would be roped in to provide the 'air bridge' to cross over large number of troops and equipment so that our Army could threaten Dacca from the eastern and southern side. Being proactive, he had already procured a large number of maps of areas beyond the Meghna River so that operations could progress towards Dacca. But before that, he had to plan to make sure that his troops reached the river banks in the first place.

From the West, the famous 'Tangail drop' was carried out by the Indian Air Force fixed wing aircraft in which 2 Para Battalion of the 50 Para Brigade was para dropped at Tangail, about 100 km west of Dacca on 11 December 1971. These 1,000 odd men and their equipment was transported by AN-12s, Fairchild Packet's, Caribou's and the Dakota's of the IAF and was one of the most successful Airborne operations since the Second World War. The retreating Pakistani troops from the North were heading towards west of Dacca so as to augment the defence of Dacca. They had to be stopped at all costs. This, however, is quite another story and has been well documented in the oft circulated stories of the 1971 war.

The Indian Eastern Army Commander, in his orders to Gen Sagat Singh had reiterated that he did not want the troops of 4 Corps to cross the Meghna River but to capture and hold the territory upto the Meghna River. But Sagat, the thinking General, had other plans which he kept close to his heart. He had realised that if he threatened Dacca, it would ensure adequate pressure on the Pakistani commanders to capitulate. Some historians have spoken about this as a 'Race to Dacca!'

This is where the role of Gp Capt Chandan Singh and the IAF helicopters came in and Air Commodore Sridharan was kind enough to share it all with me.

GP CAPT CHANDAN SINGH AND THE PLAN

Gp Capt Chandan Singh was the Station Commander at Jorhat and made in-charge of helicopter and transport operations in the eastern theatre. He was in touch with all the top army brass since a lot of flying under his command was being carried out by both the helicopter and fixed wing aircraft in support of the army.

An extremely quick thinker and charismatic leader, he got along very well with the commanders in the area of operations. Well before the war started, Chandan Singh had envisaged the use of large size helicopter troop insertions into Bangladesh to assist the Indian army if war was declared to free East Pakistan. He had full support of the Eastern Air Command HQ at Shillong and was appointed as the overall 'Task Force Commander' (TFC) for the special ops being envisaged. Therefore, he was able to take on the spot decisions.

In the words of Doc Sir, 'I think it was sometime in October or November that my CO Sqn Ldr CS Sandhu and Flight Commander Flt Lt PK Vaid went to the Corps HQ to meet General Sagat Singh. The idea to lift 57 Infantry Division by helicopters was discussed here and Chandan was left to do the detailed planning for the same.'

'This requirement had already been visualised by Chandan earlier and we had commenced training on Special Heliborne Operations (SHBO) with some of the army units well before this meeting took place.'

After the meeting, orders were received by the CO to train the unit pilots on SHBO by night since Chandan envisaged that it would be much safer, both for the aircraft and the troops to be dropped into the area teeming with Pakistani military.

'Gp Capt Chandan Singh was an amazing leader and was a great source of motivation for the young pilots who were getting ready to taste blood for the first time. He flew in and out of Agartala where the helicopters were located and saw to it that the missions were planned to the T.'

THE SQUADRON AND ITS AIRCRAFT

'We were 20 of us posted to the squadron and had no experience in actual operations except the few on the top.' The unit had been augmented by pilots who had just returned from Russia after training on the Mi-8 helicopter which was soon to be inducted to replace the ageing Mi-4. 'But our CO had so much confidence in our abilities that he decided to use us, the younger lot, for the operations,' says Doc Sir gleefully.

The Mi-4 was a piston engine helicopter with its engine in the nose section just below the cockpit. 'The only navigation aid it had was a radio compass and we were required to fly low level for all the missions even inside our own territory. Navigation was not much of a problem since the area was riverine and these rivers helped us to get from one place to the other, provided we got to the correct one!' reminisces the veteran. The night operations were generally done in bright moonlight which did not hamper the navigation and landings much at unprepared surfaces.

The Mi-4 was a Soviet design medium-lift helicopter designed to carry 1,600 kgs of weight or 16 troops and had a max range of 500 km at typical speeds of 140 to 160 kmph. The helicopters could be loaded up to the maximum since the sortie durations were not more than an hour or so, and the missions could be flown with lesser fuel in the tanks.

The Chetak helicopters were provided by the 'Kilo flight' which operated with some of the pilots of the Pakistan Air Force who had defected to our side.

Some additional Chetak helicopters were also augmented by machines from 115 Helicopter Unit at Tezpur for the recce missions.

'Wherever we operated during the war, we stayed in whatever accommodation was available close to the aircraft and we just had to open our "hold-alls" on the floor to get some sleep as and when we found the time to do so. Food was also secondary. We ate when we got things to eat and sometimes in the heat of the operations, we forgot whether we had eaten or not.' remembers Sridharan.

THE BEGINNING OF THE END

The war started on the western front on 3 December and we were also all fired up and ready by then. We were soon ready in our overalls with our bed-rolls and pistols with 6 rounds slung around our waist and awaiting further orders.

The first operational missions into East Pakistan by the IAF was by the pilots of Kilo flight.

One Chetak helicopter was tasked to carry out recce of probable landing sites in the general area of Sylhet. The CO, Flight Commander, Gp Capt Chandan Singh and Gen Sagat went for the recce. The sortie was flown at low levels and several places identified. While they were orbiting over the area, the Pakistanis realised that the aircraft was not their own and let go a volley of fire. One of the bullets grazed the General's hand and one injured Fg Offr GPS Sidhu, the co-pilot, in the leg. The helicopter was quickly flown back to Agartala, and after landing, they found that the aircraft had been peppered with 38 bullet holes!

It had been a providential escape for all the five occupants of the aircraft as no bullet found its mark at any of its vital components!

On ground after landing, all looked quite shaken but Gen Sagat was as cool as he always was. He instructed that the Chetak be checked for flight worthiness and asked for Sidhu to be evacuated to the hospital at Teliamura. Sidhu, thereafter, could not take part in the war as he recuperated in hospital.

'The Landing Grounds had been selected during this eventful sortie and this episode made us all the more determined to press on with the task at hand.'

The war plans of the unit required eight aircraft to be positioned at Corps HQ at Teliamura. The rest of the serviceable machines were to be flown to different helipads in the corps zone to be 'dispersed' so as to remain safe from enemy air attacks. Doc sir was involved in ferrying these machines to these locations along with its ground crew, and having completed this task, he was to join his team at Teliamura.

Sridharan reached Teliamura on the afternoon of 7 December and got briefed for the missions now being undertaken to Sylhet by his unit from a small airfield at Kailashaher. By the time he took off from Teliamura and landed at Kailashaher, the first mission to Syhlet had already taken off and was, in fact on its way back after dropping the troops of 4/5 Gurkhas.

'I had to wait until 1000 hours the next day (8 December) to do my first mission into East Pakistan. I was detailed as the number 3 in a three aircraft formation which was to carry 36 troops and some mortars and ammunition to Syhlet. Some enemy fire had been encountered during the first day missions and the crew was therefore briefed that the offloading had to be fast and swift so as to minimize time on ground. The troops also were also briefed the same and got some time to practice for it.'

'But the problem in my aircraft was that I was carrying the heavy loads which would entail extra time on ground for offloading. The troops on board my helicopter assured me that they would be quick and I shouldn't worry. We landed at Sylhet, offloaded, and were off the ground in a few minutes. In the next 35 minutes, the helicopter was back to the safe confines of our base. My first mission was over and it had been successful!' says Doc sir.

Sridharan flew five sorties on his first day at work in

war. Three by day and two by night. He remembers every moment spent on the missions till today.

The unit had been successful in putting across 4/5 GR (Gorkha Rifles) into Sylhet in Phase 1 of the operations. A total of 649 troops of the Gorkha Battalion were successfully inserted into Syhlet along with 13,000 kg of their load.

'These boys were so motivated and fired up to fight the enemy that as they jumped to the ground one could hear their war cry *JAI MAA KALI! AYO GORKHALI!* (Hail goddess Mahakali, the Gorkhas are here) over the din of the running engines and rotors which, by no means, were silent!' says the veteran.

4/5 Gurkha Rifles, with support from other arms, was able to demolish the resistance at the Syhlet Garrison in the next few days.

'On our way back, we inevitably had to get back some of the boys who had been injured. Bleeding and badly wounded, they would still manage a smile and one could still see that the fight hadn't gone out of them.'

'Almost all our aircraft got a few bullets holes and these were quickly repaired by our most efficient technical crew who ensured that the requisite number of machines were always available for ensuing missions.'

SUBSEQUENT MISSIONS

The first day missions for Doc sir had brought in a fair

amount of adrenalin rush which made him ready and confident for the subsequent missions. The unit was now tasked to carry out further troop insertions across the Meghna River so as to tighten the noose around Dacca and force a surrender at the earliest.

This is the first time in the history of the Helicopter Fleet of the IAF that Special Heliborne Operations (SHBO) were carried out by night. Now that the crews had gone through a few, their confidence levels were high and they were enthusiastic to go for the rest of the missions.

SHBO by night requires much superior piloting skills and has its own risks especially when being done in dark nights without any ambient lighting. Navigation is difficult and the stress levels for making the time over target as well as making the correct DZ (Dropping Zone) are high. The makeshift grounds from where the helicopters were taking off and landing in enemy territory had no landing aids but for a few 'goosenecks' and 'glim lamps' that were placed around the landing ground. These had to be made ready by our own troops available on ground. Also, some degree of protection of the area from enemy attack was required.

'As the troops kept coming in, the LZ (Landing Zone) security became less of a problem', remembers the veteran. 'Despite all this, we did suffer a few bullet hits over the next few days. Luckily for us, these were

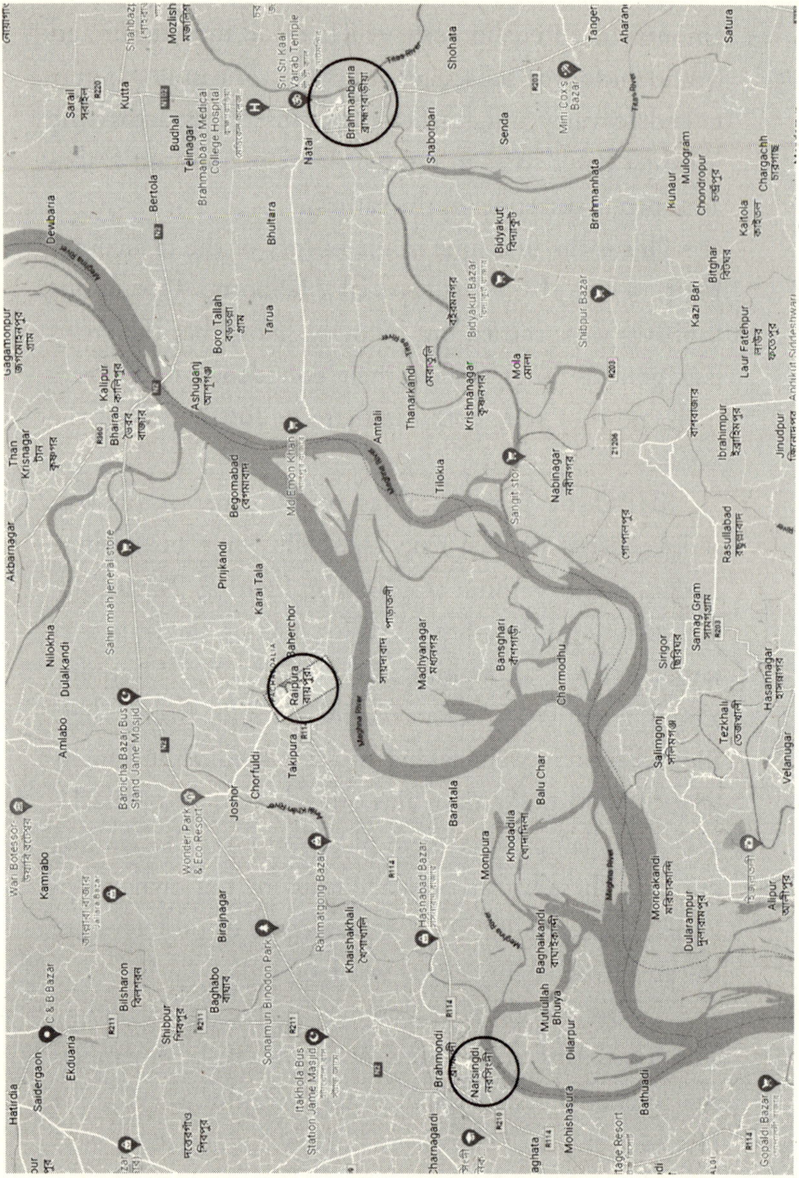

Brahmanbaria, Raipura and Narsingdi across the Meghna River.

minor injuries to the aircraft and our ground crew did an excellent job of keeping all the 10 helicopters serviceable for the missions.'

Having flown more modern machines than the Mi-4 and done SHBO by night using the modern gadgetry, I can well imagine the high level of training and confidence these young men had achieved at that point in time. In night SHBOs today, one can fly on Night Vision Goggles in almost zero light conditions and can land in restricted places. But in those times, little portable equipment like the Glim Lamps and goosenecks were required to land at night at unprepared landing grounds. Also, the remote landing strips did require these to be lit up manually all along their length for night operations to be carried out. Today, we have LED lights and the likes for this purpose which are easy to deploy.

Glim lamps are little portable battery-operated lights that can barely be seen from the air, whereas 'Goosenecks' are oil filled lamps with large wicks which can continue to burn bright for a long time. But, with the rotor downwash, these tended to extinguish as the first of the helicopters landed. As the aircraft landed one behind the other, there was no time to light them again. So, it was the little bit of ambient light and lots of skill that was needed to accomplish what they did.

Secondly, since the flights are undertaken without external lights, (those red and green lights as well as the flashing beacons) it becomes difficult for the trailing aircraft to maintain formation. Luckily for the crew undertaking these missions, the weather was good and the moon was shining bright which made things a bit easy.

PHASES OF OPERATIONS

The helicopters were positioned from Agartala to Brahmanbaria in East Pakistan which was now held by our own troops. In Phase 2 and 3 of the operations, the helicopters were required to lift troops from Brahmanbaria to Raipura and Narsingdi across the Meghna River.

The distance to the Landing Zones (LZs) was between 25 to 40 km and meant flying over enemy territory for about 30-35 min. 'While we flew at treetop heights most of the time, the threat from small arms could not be ruled out. We also had to be careful while flying over the water bodies since the Pakistanis were known to have gunboats patrolling along them,' remembers Doc Sir.

Sorties began on the 10th morning for Phase 2 and 3 of the operations and continued non-stop till the 12th. 'In three days, we had got across the Meghna river 2,856 troops and delivered almost 1,13,000 kgs of military hardware to help our boys fight the war to Dacca.'

The artillery (arty) wheeled guns were the most problematic to carry. They took a long time to load and offloading required ramps to be put at the rear to wheel them out of the cabin. This meant more time on ground in enemy territory.

In Doc Sir's words, 'Our crew and the Army guys trained on the job, and were very good. They developed excellent understanding amongst themselves and ensured that we spent least time on ground. For some reason, with my luck, I always got an arty gun to carry. While the other choppers of the formation went back as soon as they disgorged their troops, I had to fly back to base alone! And yes, the locals came in large numbers to help us offload. They were willing to brave the bullets for a good cause!'

'On the way back, we always had injured soldiers to be carried to safety. We also heard from them how the retreating Pakistanis weren't sparing the locals. Besides the looting and mass rapes being carried out, the Pakistanis were on a killing spree.'

A large number of Mukti Bahini soldiers had been found with their hands tied behind their backs and shot in their heads. 'The Pakistanis were not very kind with our soldiers too. Similar treatment was meted out to some of our guys,' remembers Sridharan.

In the fourth phase, operations shifted south to a place called Daudkhandi. 'From here we were to carry troops and equipment to Baidya Bazar, just south of Dacca. On 14 and 15 December, we carried about 2,400 troops and 73 tonnes of equipment into the area. Once again, the operations went off very smoothly and we were happy that barring a few bullet holes, we were all in one piece to take the war further.'

As they finished the operations on 15 December, word was already in that the Pakistanis were capitulating and some kind of peace and surrender was in the offing.

'We had helped the Army to tighten the noose around Dacca. There was no way that the enemy could give us a fight anymore, or so it seemed. The task force commander, Chandan Singh came over to us and gave us all a pat on the back for a job well done.'

He briefed us before he left, 'The war will now be fought on the streets of Dacca. Get ready for increased intensity in fighting from now on. These are going to be dangerous missions and we should be ready for the worst. So, keep your wits about you, don't get over confident and get ready for some hot action!'

Thankfully, this was not to happen. The Pakistanis agreed to an unconditional surrender which was to be held at Dacca Race Course on the evening of 16 December, 1971.

'We breathed a sigh of relief. War had taken a fair amount of toll on our nerves and we longed for some relief. We were glad we had ended up on the winning side and that there was a lot to cheer about.'

There was a lot to cheer about Col Behl of the Arty Regiment who fired the first shot into the Dacca Garrison on 13 December from one of the Guns dropped by the

IAF. The impact of the subsequent shelling was too much for the Pakistanis to handle.

During the entire operations, the IAF lost one helicopter but the crew were safe. The enemy, thankfully, can't claim to have a hand in this loss.

'While returning to Kumbigram from the operation area for major servicing, one helicopter had an emergency of "transmission failure" light coming on and the crew landed in an open field. While they were switching off the machine, a fire in the engine compartment was noticed which quickly engulfed the helicopter. While the crew ran to safety, the aircraft was completely gutted,' the veteran tells me.

'You see, we had been landing on unprepared grounds for a fair amount of time. A lot of dried grass was being sucked into the engine compartment. Although it was being cleaned before every flight, I suspect that the fire was due to some of this grass igniting due to the hot engine which quickly spread, and in the absence of any firefighting close by, we had to lose the machine.'

'Our technical and logistic crew did an excellent job through the short duration of the war. The serviceability state was kept high and we never had an instance of a machine not being available for flying. The fuel and oils, which are expended quite rapidly, had to be brought to the forward operating grounds and supplied to us in time. This was also the time when a lot of innovations and *jugaads* were done so that we could achieve our task.'

'For quick refueling of the aircraft, gasoline was brought in drums and we used the integral booster pumps of the aircraft itself for rapid refueling. The bullet holes had to be fixed before every flight with metallic skin patched to the aircraft skin with rivets. The technicians also needed to carry out a thorough check of the components under the skin. You see, a bullet could pierce the skin easily, hit a component and ricochet into some other component damaging it. There are millions of wires and tubes running inside the aircraft and these could be easily damaged.'

Now that the war was over, it was time to carry out routine maintenance of the helicopters and get back to the regular maintenance plans and schedules.

But before that, almost all the helicopters were required for one last important mission. 8 helicopters were required to take the big-wigs to Dacca for the surrender ceremony.

I asked Sridharan sir to narrate me his version of the surrender ceremony.

'The entire victory formation of 8 helicopters was ready for take-off with our CO Charu Sandhu fittingly in the lead. It was late afternoon on 16 December that we set course for Dacca—a mere 40 minutes away from Agartala. It was a bright and clear day as all choppers navigated their way to Dacca for the Grand Finale. The outbound flight was uneventful. We flew low across all the territory that our forces had captured and recognised the places we had clandestinely flown to—on the many operational missions—in the last few days.'

'As we approached Dacca, Nanda asked me if I could spot the Dacca Golf Course close to the Kurmitola Airfield. As he was an avid golfer, seeing a golf course excited him to no end! I wasn't too fond of the game though.'

'Further ahead, I spotted the Tezgaon Dacca Airfield, and as we approached it, we saw the big craters made by our Fighters and Bombers. Because of complete air superiority over Bangladesh, we had been able to operate with impunity and achieve our goals with ease. This had also allowed our Army operations to continue unhindered. This Air Superiority that we held from the second day of Operation "Cactus Lily" helped our Armed Forces to speed up Operation "Jackpot" to seize East Pakistan and force Gen Niazi and the Pakistani Army to lay down their arms on 16 December.'

'We saw the reception party on ground and adjusted to land one by one with our CO leading the way. Once on ground, all 8 helicopters switched off and the Pakistani entourage led by Gen Niazi and Farman Ali came forward to receive our 3 Service Heads led by Gen JS Aurora.'

'There was loud cheering by the locals as we all were

herded into different cars and vehicles to be taken to Dacca Race Course. Nanda, Carriappa and I were in an open Jeep as we rushed towards the ground. The road was lined with Bangladeshi crowds and as we drove, we saw the ravages of the war caused by our Air Force and Army. By the time we reached the huge Race Course ground, it was early evening and the Surrender Ceremony was soon to start with all the dignitaries gathering around the tables that had been laid out by our jawans.'

'Gen Niazi took his Seat along with the civilian Governor and across the table sat Gen Arora. All the other Commanders of all 3 Services crowded around the table with Surrender Document in front of them. There was plenty of pushing, pulling and jostling going on as everyone wanted to be eye-witness to what was going on at the table. Whilst I wasn't so lucky to get near the table, only Flying Officer 'Kruts' Krishnamurthy managed to bulldoze his way amongst the VIPs. He literally pushed Gen JFR Jacob, the Eastern Command Chief of Staff to one side to get a ringside view! It would have been quite a story if the man who negotiated the surrender with Gen Niazi had been pushed out of the picture!'

'Wild cheering erupted as the Signing Ceremony started. I spent time talking to some new BAF officers who gave graphic accounts of the cruelties of the Pakistani Army and the bravery of the Indian Army's soldiers as they moved into the streets of Dacca. They wanted us to stay back and celebrate the victory alongside them.'

'But we had to get back to the Dacca airfield to return to Agartala after these historic moments that we all would cherish for our entire lives. A new nation—Bangladesh was born and we had helped in our own little way in creating this new country.'

As the sun settled in the west and light faded rapidly, the entire lot of VIPs in the eight aircraft was safely back on ground in India. All of them, in their own way, had played a significant role in liberating the people of East Pakistan from the clutches of tyranny —happy to be part of the history of both the Nations.

But there were so many more—so many who could not come to the ceremony but their contribution to the victory cannot be ignored. Be it the men in greens, the IAF pilots, the technical support crews, the cooks, waiters, dhobi's, lascars and the barmen and everybody else who worked tirelessly in the background. Each of them had their little roles to play in the victory and the victory was theirs as much as for the ones who got down from the aircrafts at Agartala.

As we parted ways, Doc Sir told me, 'As promised, we did attend the New Year celebrations in Dacca Intercontinental and can never forget the day when we said adieu to the most happening year of our lives! That is, of course, another story for another time!'

THE RAJPUT CAVALIER

AIR VICE-MARSHAL CHANDAN SINGH

In the past few stories in this book, the name of Chandan Singh has cropped up many times. In my opinion, if it hadn't been for General Sagat and Group Captain Chandan Singh, the outcome of the 1971 war would have been different. I decided to get in touch with his son, Sajjan Singh, who kindly agreed to tell me of some anecdotal history about his father through many of their family and friends.

Here's a hero of 1971 about whom not much has been written about after the war. His biography titled *A Cavalier in the Sky* written by Major Chandra Kant Singh, their family friend, has just been released after his death last year on 29 March, 2021. It takes us through the extraordinary life of the Air Marshal and the Indian Air Force of those times. I did manage to get in touch with Maj Chandrakant Singh who gave me some inputs for this story.

Chandra Kant and Chandan met each other on board a Chetak helicopter while they carried out a recce being planned for the Special Heliborne Operations (SHBO) to put troops across the Meghana River in the first week of war. 'Squadron Leader Pushp Vaid was flying the Chetak carrying out the recce while Chandan and I looked around for possible landing sites,' says the octogenarian.

'I realised what a great leader he was by the way he took decisions to undertake the most-risky of missions. After the war, Chandan "adopted" me as his son and we would often sit discussing what all happened during the war,' says the veteran, now settled in Jodhpur, the place where Chandan too lived his retired life.

'That day, we came back with a lot of bullet holes and the co-pilot, Flying Officer Sidhu was also injured. An unperturbed Chandan had asked Vaid to arrange for Sidhu's evacuation and went about the planning of the exercise with General Sagat Singh as if nothing had happened.'

'I wish he had been alive at the launch of his biography, the world would have got to meet the great man in person!' says his son Sajjan, who runs the family business and also keenly follows history—especially IAF history.

Born on 3 December, 1925 at Bagawas near Jodhpur, Chandan was initially recruited in the 'Jodhpur Lancers' as a Second Lieutenant when he was just 16. Having fought World War II in Iraq, Palestine, Iran, and Egypt as a foot soldier, he was motivated by Maharaja Umed Singh to join the Royal Indian Air Force. Umed, incidentally, had been conferred with the rank of an Air Marshal by the Royal Air Force.

Chandan was initially commissioned as a fighter pilot flying the Spitfires, but had to move to fly transport aircraft due to an accident. He served the IAF for thirty-four years before he retired in 1980 as an Air Vice Marshal. For his bravery and leadership in war, he was decorated with the Vir Chakra in 1965 and the Mahavir Chakra in 1971. Besides, he was the also recipient of the Ati Vishisht Seva Medal (AVSM) and the Vishisht Seva Medal (VSM) for meritorious service.

Sajjan describes an incident soon after the surrender ceremony at Dacca. Someone asked a very somber General Niazi as to why he decided to yield so soon—without a fight. Niazi was in no mood to talk and walked towards a senior IAF officer standing nearby and tapped the 'wings' on his uniform. That senior officer was, in fact, Chandan.

'Whether he meant IAF action or my father's bravery

is not clear, but in any case, my father was responsible for most of the air action that happened in the east and I would like to believe that Niazi meant my father!' says Sajjan.

'My earliest memory of my father is of 1967. It was a late marriage and I was barely two when dad became a Wing Commander. I remember him waving out to me every day when I went to school. Soon, he was a Group Captain and we moved to Jorhat where he was to command the important transport base.'

A mosquito infested station with not much of infrastructure, Jorhat was important because most of the transport support operations for the north east of the country were being undertaken from there.

'By the time Dad was posted out, Jorhat was shining with major changes in living conditions. He established a poultry, fishery, piggery, dairy and what not to make the base self-reliant—even the mosquito menace was controlled by use of the citronella plant that grew wild along the runway! Jorhat was later chosen to hold the Investiture Ceremony and Presidential Parade largely due to his efforts.'

'Jorhat was like one big family. It was a simple yet happy life. We, children, unabashedly went to each other's homes, played, ate and slept together.' Being a young boy, Sajjan had no clue what his father was up to in the run up to the war. 'I thought he did a desk job since he went with a briefcase every morning and came back late in his staff car. Sometimes he would disappear for a few days and we were told he was away to meet "Lal" Uncle or "Sagat" Uncle (Air Chief Marshal PC Lal and Lt Gen Sagat Singh). I remember the time when they both came home to meet the family over a cup of tea a few times.'

'We learned many years later about Kilo Flight and Daddy's role in training the Pakistani pilots in Dimapur and laying the foundation for the future Bangladesh Air Force (BAF). Daddy never, or extremely rarely, spoke about his role and achievements in the IAF, but I do remember him saying, "We did what we had to do in the amount of time that we had—I don't understand what all the hoopla is about?" And I would answer, "They didn't award you the Maha Vir Chakra (MVC) and Vir Chakra (VrC) for nothing." Daddy would just shrug his shoulders and smile. That was truly one of his greatest qualities.'

In his retired years, Chandan and his brother Brig Hari Singh, AVSM, would sit down and discuss the war threadbare, discussing tactics and strategy and what all could have been done and what was not done. 'Whenever I sat down to listen, they would smile and change the topic! I did, however, often hear the story of the Paramvir Chakra (PVC) hero of Rezangla—Maj Shaitan Singh.'

'Despite being a year older than Daddy, Shaitan joined school late and was my uncle Brig Hari Singh's classmate. They were bench-mates at school and trained together to join the Jodhpur State Forces together. Both my uncle and Maj Shaitan Singh were outstanding sportspersons and the discussions would veer off towards sports more often than not when he was around.'

'Dad would also narrate how he had flown the Major to Rezangla straight from hospital where he was recovering from a frost bite. I was so mesmerized by the simple tales of their valour, and would often day dream of being one of them when I grew up!'

'I met General Sagat Singh a few times not just in Jorhat but even after his retirement at his home, aptly named "Meghna," in Jaipur. He was still a tall and imposing man. He and Daddy got along extremely well for many reasons. They had many things common between them—the harsh deserts of Rajasthan, the humble backgrounds, both were in the State Forces before Independence, and their liking of each other's company! Most importantly, because of Daddy being a Cavalry man before joining the Air Force, it was easier for him to understand the "army mind" of the legendary General.'

Chandan had commenced writing about his life in his autobiography which ran into more than 300 pages a few years ago. 'When we, his children, prodded him to get it into print, he simply tore off the entire manuscript! He reasoned that no one would be interested in knowing about his life and it was not worth the effort to get the story into a book form.'

'Whenever asked about his life in the IAF, he would clam up and refuse to answer questions,' says Major Chandra Kant. It took years of persistent efforts and patience on the part of Chandra Kant to get the biography *Cavalier in the Sky* in print, albeit a bit late.

'I do not think that I will be able to add any more to what has been written by Major Chandra Kant,' says Sajjan when I asked him if he thought of writing something on his father.

'How has it been to be the son of one of the great warriors of the IAF?'

'In the beginning it was hard to be Daddy's son as friends and relatives expected so much from me! It was like a heavy stone on my head, but as the years went by, this feeling took a 180 degree turn. I realised that people treated me and my family with a lot of respect and many hurdles that the family faced were sorted out just because of him!'

Chandan today is remembered by people who know him as the person who paid for their children's education, a person who got them jobs and the one who motivated them to join the Armed Forces, thus, changing their lives for the better. 'Till a month before he passed away, he ensured that a large part of his pension was distributed to accounts of girls wanting to study and their welfare. After retirement, he ensured that weaker sections were employed in large numbers in our limestone quarry business.'

Chandan disliked politics in the Armed Forces and often spoke his mind about the continued interference of civilians in military matters. Being a voracious reader right till his end, he was clued up about what was happening not only in India but the world too.

'My father could connect with the young and old alike—so flexible a personality was he. All those who met him know how easy he was to get along with and they often approached him for advice on matters troubling them. He was instrumental in getting my son into the army by training him for the exams and the interview. He is now a Major in the Army and I hope he will be able to follow the footsteps of his grandfather!'

'What about your mother?' I ask him.

'My mother was a big support to Daddy. It wasn't easy for her as she came from a very different background, and it took time for her to adjust to the IAF way of life. But she did it so well and fulfilled her role of an IAF officer's wife in all respects. Though her "Air Force life" lasted only about 17 years, since Dad retired after that, she is fondly remembered by all who got to know her at Aviation Research Centre (ARC) Charbatia, Jorhat, the United Kingdom, Delhi and Allahabad.'

'Do you remember the days of the war when dad was away?' I enquire further. 'A funny incident occurred during the war. The Chinese radio announced that they had captured Daddy and even gave his full name and service details, as if they had got the information from him during interrogation. We were told it was propaganda to demoralise our troops fighting on the eastern front. When we tried to find out more from the radio and newspapers, mysteriously, the lights would go off during the broadcasts and the newspapers also did not reach our doorstep for many days.' The family was disturbed and waited for some official confirmation which never came.

What happened after a few days was more surprising. One day while the children were returning from school in the 'Shaktiman' school bus, it made an unscheduled halt midway from home. 'Our names were announced and we were asked to get off the bus. And when we got down blinking our eyes due to the bright sun, we saw Daddy standing there with open arms and his eyes shining even brighter than the sun! It was a very emotional moment and a happy one at that which is still so fresh in my mind!'

When the legend passed away in March 2020, Covid-19 protocols had been strictly enforced. Yet, so many people managed to come for the funeral to pay their respects. 'The IAF provided the hearse and escort, and condolence messages were received from our PM Narendra Modi as well as the Defence Minister Rajnath Singh. Others, who sent their personal messages, included Gajendra Singh Shekhawat, Jal Shakti Minister and MP from Jodhpur, the CM of Rajasthan Shri Ashok Gehlot, Sachin Pilot, (whose father had served under Daddy) former CM Vasundhara Raje, CDS General Bipin Rawat, IAF chief Air Chief Marshal RKS Bhadauria, the Chief of the Bangladesh Air Force and a host of others. It was so heartening to see that so many people from different walks of life remembered the soldier.'

'He made a name where ever he was posted and left a legacy to be adored, followed and emulated.'

'Daddy was awarded the Mahavir Chakra (MVC) for his role in 1971 War and the medal is proudly displayed at his home in Jodhpur.'

His citation for the MVC goes thus:

> *Group Captain Chandan Singh, AVSM, VrC is the officer commanding of an Air Force Station in the East. During the war with Pakistan, he was in the forefront of the air operations conducted for the liberation of Bangladesh. Group Captain Chandan Singh was also responsible for the planning and execution of the special helicopter operations to airlift two companies of troops in the Sylhet area. When it became necessary to overcome the obstacles in the advance of the army towards Dacca, he planned and executed the move of nearly 3,000 troops and 40 tons of equipment and heavy guns with the extremely limited helicopter force at his disposal. This operation entailed landing the troops and equipment near heavily defended areas by*

> *night. Prior to each mission he personally carried out reconnaissance in the face of heavy enemy fire. On the night of December 7/8, he flew eight missions, deep into enemy territory to supervise the progress of the helicopter airlift and to guide and inspire his pilots who were facing heavy opposition from ground fire. Later, he flew another 18 missions in the same operation, always leading from the front. On many occasions his helicopter was hit by ground fire, but this did not deter him from achieving the aim. The success of this major airborne operation contributed significantly to the fall of Dacca and the capitulation of the Pakistan Armed Forces, in Bangladesh. The leadership, drive and determination coupled with the bravery shown by Group Captain Chandan Singh over an extended period of time, are in the highest traditions of the Air Force.*

'Any last words?' I ask the man who has shared so much of his father's life with me.

'Being the son of a legend is both a problem and blessing!'

'A problem since people expect so much from me, not realising that I am Daddy's son and not him! It's hard! It's a blessing, since wherever I go, I am recognised and introduced to others as "AVM Sahab's son!" and people become friendly and chatty after that. I am stuck somewhere in the labyrinths of government departments, a mention of Daddy's name eases things out.'

'The best thing about being his son is that I get to hear amazing stories of him and his friends, stories that he would never have told me otherwise! Some are still classified, whilst others are in the process of being declassified by the US and Indian government. Someday perhaps, these would be in public domain.'

'If Daddy would have been serving in the modern IAF of today, just the thought of how he would have done things that he did with the now available modern war fighting equipment available is exciting and fires my imagination!'

EJECTION BEHIND ENEMY LINES

AIR CMDE JAWAHAR LAL BHARGAVA

This is the story of then Flying Officer and now Air Commodore Jawahar Lal Bhargava, Fighter Pilot, a 1971 war veteran.

Commissioned into the Indian Air Force in March 1963, he underwent his flying training in the 83rd Course at the Air Force Academy, then located at Jodhpur. In 1965, as a young Flying Officer with barely a few years of service, Bhargava was sent to the US to undergo an advanced fighter gunnery course. In April '69, while flying the Mystere aircraft, he had multiple bird hits which crippled the engine of his aircraft, forcing him to eject. He recovered soon enough and was soon fit to fly, and, in 1971, he was posted at the 220 Squadron, flying the indigenous HF-24 Marut.

Later in 1971, while flying his first sortie over enemy territory, his aircraft was shot by the enemy Air Defence, and he had to eject the second time, only to land up in the Pakistani hands as a POW. After spending nearly a year in various Pakistani jails, he was sent back to India on 1 December 1972. The tenacious officer was soon back to flying fighters and served the IAF for 32 long years, post which he retired and settled in Panchkula near Chandigarh.

At 80, the veteran displays an elephantine memory from which he pulls out some stories of the 1971 war in the western sector.

'I was finally in solitary confinement. It had been an arduous seven to eight-day journey and my back hurt due to the injury aggravated by the rough camel and jeep rides. The journey with my captors had begun from the crash site close to Vasarbha (15 km west of Khokropar in Pakistan) and reached somewhere in the heart of Rawalpindi about 700 km from our national capital. In between, I had landed up at Drigh Road in Karachi—the birthplace of our Indian Air Force.'

His aircraft had been left smoldering and in pieces close to the place he had landed using his parachute. By now, eight days later, the metal would have turned cold and be lying half buried in the sands of the majestic Thar desert. Maybe, inquisitive boys from nearby villages would have searched around the crash site for interesting pieces of the aircraft to be kept as war trophies.

'En route, we had numerous halts for interrogation and change of transport. It was during these halts that I got a whiff of where I was, since my handcuffs were removed and my eyes unmasked. A hot and sweet cup of tea along with something to eat was almost always available and welcome. Wherever we ran into a doctor, I requested him for pain killers to ease the discomfort in my back and spine which made this journey just about bearable.'

As the sun went down in Rawalpindi, a small wattage bulb illuminated his dingy room revealing a thin mattress covering a jute stringed cot. The prison had been kind to give him a thin pillow and a blanket for whatever it was worth to counter the chill of winter.

Very soon, Bhargava realised that he wasn't alone at this prison. There were more captured pilots like him who he was to meet later. 'We were at the mercy of the guard stationed outside the cell to be permitted to go to common loo to ease ourselves.' With his stomach showing signs of frequent failure due to the poor quality of intake, the need to go to this cold, dark and smelly dungeon was that much more.

Bhargava Sir is 80 and still remembers those days of the war and the aftermath clearly. He was willing to give me a blow-by-blow account of his adventurous journey in Pakistan and his life thereafter.

'I was born in Pataudi, a small town in the present district of Gurugram on the outskirts of Delhi. The place is well known for the Nawab of Pataudi-Junior, his father, Mohammad Iftikhar Ali Khan Siddiqui Pataudi (IAK Pataudi) and their grand palace called the "Ibrahim Kothi." Our family was close to the royals, and I spent many an hour playing with Mansoor, who, like his father, went on to captain the Indian cricket team. Mansoor's real uncle, Sher Ali Khan, migrated to Pakistan and became a General in their Army!'

'You must be wondering why am I telling you all this? Well, this relation with the Pataudi family was to help me to survive in 1971, and you will soon know how when I finish my story!' he keeps me in suspense with a chuckle.

'I remember playing with Mansoor at his home and also got to meet many VIPs of those times who came visiting. Most probably, Mansoor, being a royal, was forbidden from eating peanuts—can't say that with certainty though. I often sneaked into the Pataudi home with peanuts in the big pockets of my shorts. And soon, Mansoor and I would be under the billiards table—our favourite hiding place, enjoying the toasted nuts and leaving remnants of our doings on the floor! We were caught soon enough, but that did not deter us from being naughty—our bond of friendship grew stronger doing things against the "Royal" grain!' Bhargava has many interesting stories about his association with the

Pataudi family but I guess it will have to wait for later.

It was the 5 December 1971 and the war was into its second day. Being unwell and not available for flying for the first two days, Bhargava was keen to get into the middle of things. He found himself planned for a morning mission on that day.

'It was a 2 aircraft strike mission in the "Naya Chor" area with my Flight Commander, Squadron Leader KK (Joe) Bakshi as my leader.'

'Right from the time we took off, I realised that my radio wasn't working too well and I could hear Joe and the ATC intermittently. I informed my leader about the problem and he asked me to continue along with him.' At short ranges, radio reception with his leader was alright but to receive the ATC and ground transmissions was difficult.

This was to prove costly later.

Whilst heading out towards the border, the Forward Air Controller (FAC), Flight Lieutenant Mulla Feroze, had given out the latest 'Forward Line of Own Troops' or the FLOT. 'Apparently, our own troops had moved almost 15 km further west into Pakistani territory. Due to the garbled radio, I didn't monitor this important information. If I had, I would have been able to walk towards our own troops and get rescued after the crash. But this was not to be.'

As the aircraft came over the target area, a large

volume of anti-aircraft fire awaited them.

In the words of the veteran, 'We were at low level into enemy territory, flying at approximately 200 feet above ground at about 900 kmph. Our targets were to be installations on the airfield at Naya Chor and other targets of opportunity like military trains, tanks and army concentrations. We were fully laden with drop tanks (extra fuel tanks under wing for added range), rockets and guns. We found nothing much in Naya Chor, but, around the airfield, we spotted some army formations whom we targeted with rockets.'

Coming in for the second attack, Bhargava's aircraft apparently was hit multiple times from ground fire. 'I was engrossed in getting into the second attack when the first hydraulic failure audio warning came on. The aircraft suddenly turned right and went into manual flying mode.'

'I have been hit!' called out Bhargava to his mate. 'Ok,' said a calm Bakshi. 'Continue turning right and head towards the border….'

Bhargava remembers the sequence of events that happened thereafter as if it had happened yesterday. 'Everything now happened in a flash. In the turn, I realised that I could not spot my leader and gave him a call only to realise that my radio had failed. Turning east, I saw my left engine RPM winding down and I immediately tried to relight (restart) it but to no avail.'

The aircraft was heavy with the drop tanks and could barely sustain flight on a single engine which was also threatening to quit with its parameters going out of limits. He decided to jettison his drop tanks to make the aircraft lighter.

'I had now descended to almost dune height, and as I passed a mosque, I appreciated how low my airspeed was and how close to the ground I was. Looking inside, I saw that my Air Speed Indicator (ASI) had also given up!'

Whilst dealing with the various emergencies that kept cropping up, Bhargava realised that his aircraft would soon stall out of control. He decided to eject.

'I pulled the standby ejection handle between my legs and nothing happened. If not now, I would have to go down with my sick aircraft!' Trying to control the aircraft with one hand on the control stick, he tried the main ejection handle located above his head. Thankfully, this time, the ejection system worked and he was out of the aircraft with a whoosh and a flash whilst his machine met its end in the dunes.

His parachute had barely opened as Bhargava landed on the soft sand of the desert right next to his aircraft. The airplane laid half buried, burning, with the rockets and ammunition inside the pods exploding every few seconds. 'I was more afraid of the locals lynching me than the shrapnel from the rockets injuring me!'

He stayed near the burning mass of metal and

fuel for the next few hours deciding his next course of action. 'I first decided to bury my parachute and took stock of what was available in my survival pack. Keeping my helmet on for protection, I rummaged through the survival pack and kept a few important things with me that would help me to subsist on my own during my walk home in hostile conditions.'

Squadron Leader Bakshi kept orbiting over the crash site for a while to look for the downed pilot. He had smoke coming out of his aircraft and things did not look too good for him too.

'I waved to him and hoped that he saw me. I imagined that he would soon send a rescue helicopter to pick me up.'

But none came.

In reality, Bakshi hadn't seen his young Number 2 and thought that he had gone down with the machine. Returning to base, he informed the base commander, 'I don't think "Brother" Bhargava has made it!' (Why he is still called 'Brother' is a long story for later!)

'I saw my leader in his smoking aircraft exiting the area after a while and kept praying that he would land back safely at base.'

Having looked through the contents of the survival pack, he realised that there wasn't an emergency map inside. 'The only map I had, had gone down with the aircraft. I did go around the crash site to see if it had survived, without luck. I was, therefore, forced to work out my position on ground with knowledge of the map I had studied before the sortie. In my estimation, I was north of the railway line, and if I headed east, I would be able to make it to the border soonest.'

'I looked at my watch which showed 0920 hours IST. I decided to change the time to PST (Pakistan Standard Time) whilst I planned my next course of action. The compass in the survival pack was a great morale booster.' It would help Bhargava to head east in the direction of safety.

An incident that happened soon after spelt his doom and subsequent capture.

Surprisingly, in the first few hours of the crash, Bhargava did not see a single human being approach the crash site or come looking for him.

'At about 1230 PST, I heard some conversation at a distance and I realised that someone was approaching. Picking up my survival pack with its reduced items, I started to run on an easterly heading leaving foot prints on the sand, for about a kilometer.'

It was difficult to run on the sand in the tight and heavy G-suit. The flying overall and the suit would also be a give-away if he was caught. Stopping to catch his breath, Bhargava removed them and threw them into some hedges close by. He was in his civvies now, which were worn under overalls for missions. He had some Pakistani currency, a few bottles of water and a knife for company.

In operational missions into enemy territory, pilots wear civilian clothes under their overalls *Salwar Kameez* in this case, so that one can merge with the local population in case of a crash in enemy territory. Pilots also carry some foreign currency which can be used if required to save oneself.

In hindsight, Bhargava feels that the men whom he heard could well have been Indian soldiers. Maybe, in a case of mistaken identity, he had run away from safety! The rescue party sent by the Indian Army recovered the buried parachute and ejection seat near the crash site and also recovered the overalls and G-suit which were promptly sent back to his squadron.

'At least, the guys back home knew that I had survived the crash!'

Later on, Mulla Feroze narrated his part of the story when they met up in jail. Flight Lieutenant Mulla Feroze and Capt Dastur were on duty as Forward Air Controller and Ground Liaison Officer in the area around Naya Chor. They both fell into Pakistani hands a few hours later.

Mulla Feroze told Bhargava that he was very close to the crash site and had seen the aircraft with its rear end in flames. He, however, hadn't seen the ejection and wasn't sure if Bhargava had survived. Both Mulla and Dastur managed to convince the local army unit Commanding Officer to send a few men to search for the downed pilot.

'In all probability, these were the men who recovered

my parachute and flying clothing and sent it to my unit. When I got back, my CO showed me my parachute which he had kept with himself while my ejection seat was lying in the squadron hangar.'

Disoriented and dehydrated, Bhargava was about to give up when he saw a village a few kilometers away. He came to a few huts at the perimeter and met an old man. 'I am Flight Lieutenant Mansoor Ali and I have just survived a crash. I need water to drink!' The first Muslim name that had come to mind was of Mansur Ali Khan Pataudi, his childhood friend! The old man indicated to a tank of water used by cattle and Bhargava got to quench his thirst to his heart's content. He also filled up his four bottles for later use.

'Is that village *Bhitala*?' asked Bhargava pointing to the village and warming up to the old man. 'No No, that is *Pirani Ki Paar*!' said the surprised man.

The realisation dawned on Bhargava. All this while, he had been terribly wrong in his mental reckoning. He was well south of where he had thought he was. 'I gave 20 rupees to the old man and requested him not to tell anyone that I had been seen.'

Bhargava now began his journey home on a new heading—towards the border hoping to catch the railway line that would help navigate to the border fastest. At about 1730 hours, while going around some dunes, he saw a Mi-4 helicopter hovering a little distance away perhaps trying to find him. He waved and shouted but was not seen. The chopper soon went away eastwards into the failing light of the dusk.

Dead tired with all that had happened through the day, Bhargava decided to slip into a man-made 8-foot trench to rest for the night.

After a little while, he was rudely awakened from his tired slumber by three men staring down at him, torches in hand.

'Who are you and what are you doing here?' A volley of questions followed before he could reply.

'I am Flight Lieutenant Mansoor Ali Khan of the Pakistani Air Force and I was shot down by the Indians near Bhitala village this morning.'

'Arre! you are very near the Indians here, come along with us and we shall get you to safety. Come! Walk with us to our village...'

'Is there any police station near your village?' asked Bhargava as they walked. He was relieved when he was told that there was none in the vicinity.

'Kitni door hai border yahan se? (How far are we from the border?),' Bhargava enquired thinking of how he was going to give them the slip. *'6 se 7 kos'* came the answer from one of them. (A Kos is equal to 1.2 miles or 1.8 km).

At the village, when Bhargava asked for help with a camel ride to Bhitala, the villagers told him that the town had been taken over by the Indians the same day.

'No No!' said Bhargava trying to outwit them. 'We have fought hard and taken back the town!' But the villagers didn't seem convinced. 'I even gave them 200 rupees for hiring a camel.'

The village school headmaster suspected something fishy about Bhargava's story and sent someone to fetch the Pakistani Rangers to come verify the 'outsider.'

And while they waited, the first of the informal interrogations started. The headmaster wanted to know where Bhargava was from and if he could provide his address. 'I am from Rawalpindi, Mall Road,' he answered confidently.

He was told that the Rangers were coming to get him in three hours. This led Bhargava into thinking of giving them the slip by around 8 pm well before the Rangers arrived. He lay on the charpoy, his back in spasms of pain, with the villagers crowding around him. He then requested for some tea. As he sipped the sweet brew, he thought of his next move. He even gave away his little belongings to the children hovering around—in a bid to gain their confidence. It was nearing eight and he requested them for another cup. Unfortunately for him, the Rangers landed up earlier than expected just around the time the second cup of tea was served, and took charge of the situation.

'Show me your watch,' said one of the rangers, taking his hand and looking at the time. 'Thankfully, I was already on PST and I managed to earn their confidence even before their interrogation started.' Being questioned was going to be the pattern for the next few days. 'They asked me if I was a devout Muslim and if I could recite the *Kalma*.' Bhargava could not even repeat the verses after they were recited aloud to him by one of the rangers. He felt the heat building and knew his game was up.

'They threatened me with dire consequences if I didn't tell the truth.'

He decided to spill the beans. 'I am 7209, Flight Lieutenant Jawahar Lal Bhargava of the Indian Air Force,' he blurted, giving out his service number as per Geneva Conventions and laying all speculations to rest. 'You can do anything to me and even kill me if you want.'

'Why are you in civil clothes?' asked a Ranger. 'I threw away my flying overalls after I landed on ground to save myself,' replied Bhargava.

'I now thought that the villagers would lynch me before the rangers took me away. Thankfully, they were nice and the village headman said, *'Arre aap hamare mehmaan hai! Agar hame pata hota ki aap us paar se aaye hain, hum aapki khatirdari karte!'* (If we knew you were our guest from the other side, we would have looked after you!)

'This raised my morale and I accepted their invitation to a meal.'

'Kya aap bada/Chhota khate hain?' I was asked. (Do you eat Buffalo/Cow meat?)

'I replied in the negative and told them that I could have chicken if they could offer the same.' And pronto, a chicken meal was arranged which all of them relished before setting course on the camels.

And while they ate, one of the villagers approached Bhargava, 'Do you want to write a letter to your Begum? I keep visiting Barmer (in Rajasthan) often, and will post it for you,' he offered.

I quickly scribbled a note to my wife which read something like this:

> *My dear,*
> *I am very sorry to disappoint you all. I am now in Pakistan and, hopefully, will be declared a POW tomorrow. Love to everybody. I am fit and fine and hope to see you soon.*

He addressed the envelope: '220 Squadron, IAF, C/O 56 APO.'

The letter of course, was never delivered.

Bhargava's journey begins at Bhitala near the crash site and continues through the towns of Chachro, Umarkot, Mirpur and Badin before going to the big city of Karachi and ending up at Rawalpindi.

The same is given in the table.

Bhargava comes out of his interesting historical narration for an interlude with a glass of water. He tells

S.NO	DATE	FROM	TO	MODE OF TRANSPORT	REMARKS
1.	05 Dec	Bhitala	Chachro	Camel back	From crash site
2.	06 Dec	Chachro	Umarkot	Open one tonner truck	
3.	07/08 Dec	Umarkot	Mirpur Khas	Jeep	
4.	09 Dec	Mirpur Khas	Badin	Jeep	
5.	10 Dec	Badin	Karachi	Jeep	At Drigh Road
6.	11 Dec	Karachi	Rawal-pindi	Propeller Aircraft	POW Camp

me, 'There are many stories about my journey and the year-long stay in Pakistani Jails which I shall recount in my biography that I plan to write soon. Let me give you a trailer and taste of some of them today!'

He dives back into history…

'These guys didn't even have handcuffs and blindfolds for me. I carried two large handkerchiefs (even now, I do!) and these were used to tie my hands together and blindfold my eyes. The worst journey was on the camel. The constant gyrations of the camel back without visual reference made my stomach churn and led to spatial disorientation. I, especially, hated the time when the camel was made to sit down and stand-up during halts.'

Once a while when they heard IAF planes overhead, Bhargava would promptly advise the entourage to get

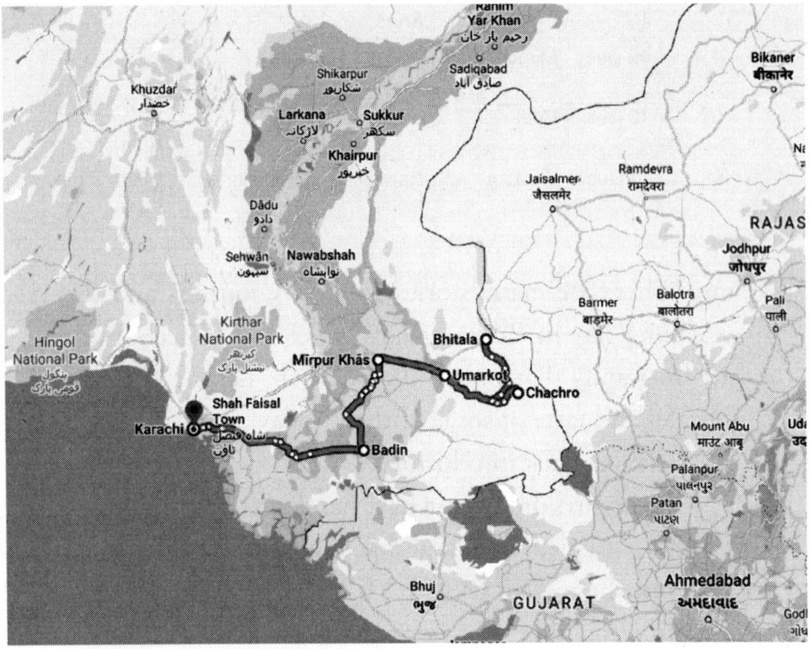

The journey from Bhitala near the crash site through the towns of Chachro, Umarkot, Mirpur and Badin before going to the big city of Karachi.

into hiding. 'I didn't want to be shot by my own friends!'

Some of the Rangers were not so friendly. They frequently needled him with questions about who he really was.

'Civil drees kyon pehna hai? (Why are you wearing a civil dress?)' they repeatedly asked. Bhargava had a hard time convincing them that he was really a downed pilot and not a spy. He showed them the 'identity disc' around his neck to prove that he, indeed, was a IAF pilot.

'Dalle nu maar goli!' (Kill the bloody pimp!) said an infuriated ranger, when he tried to reassure them that he wasn't a spy. 'I think it was their leader Awaz Ali (I think he was a Havildar) who prevented me from getting shot by pacifying his men. For the first few hours of the camel ride, I was constantly in fear of a bullet coming in from behind.'

En route, they stopped at an Army camp where a very pleasant Captain received Bhargava and offered him tea and biscuits. 'I complained to him that the Rangers had threatened to shoot me.'

'We have been looking for you! You are now in safe hands and would be handed over to the Pakistani Army authorities tomorrow!' he told a relieved Bhargava.

'On the way to Chachro on camel on the same day, near a small village, one of my escorts asked me if I needed a water break. I was in no mood to go through the motions of the camel sitting down and getting up and I refused, saying that we should move on. Another Ranger, however, said he wanted a halt and halt they did.'

'It was late evening and I heard them speaking with the villagers rather loudly. One of the villagers was telling them, *"Chachro hindustani fauj le gayi hai!* (Chachro has been taken over by the Indian forces!)" *"Yeh kaisa ho sakta hai!"* exclaimed our leader and the rangers got into a discussion.'

Chachro, indeed, had been taken by the brave soldiers of the 10 Para Commando's (Desert Scorpions) of our Army. Their famous commanding officer, Lt Col Bhavani Singh of the royal family of Jaipur had led his troops in one of the most daring and stealthy surgical strikes during the war and taken over the Pakistani positions without losing a single man.

Bhargava and his captors, therefore, abandoned their plan to proceed further and the group stayed at the village that night.

'What if we hadn't stopped for a break? The captors would have been taken captive, my camel ride would have ended and I would have been a free man! But that is destiny and one can't change things that happened in the past!' chuckles the veteran.

'Oh, the Camel! I had started hating this animal by now and prayed to god for this part of the journey to be over!'

The camel ride finally ended on the evening of 7

December. 'I was bundled into a blanket and shoved into a small hut for the night. I heard the Rangers telling the snoopy villagers that I was a senior officer in custody and wasn't to be disturbed.' Later on, he came to know that the Rangers were taking no chances since the area that they camped for the night had a sizeable Hindu population.

Next morning, the now 'POW' was handed over to one Captain Murtaza of the Pakistani Army in the middle of the desert.

'We were to spend the day at camp itself till Murtaza received orders from "above." Murtaza was a courteous man and allowed my handcuffs and blindfold to be removed. With a stern warning, he allowed me to roam about the little camp area. There was no food for anyone and we survived on several cups of tea and cigarettes. His Jonga had five-star interiors and I realised how much power the Pakistani officers wielded and also the lavish lifestyle they led. Come evening, Bhargava was loaded into the rear of a one-tonner truck and driven for about two hours to Umarkot. "It was bitingly cold and despite the two blankets provided, I was frozen to the bone at the end of the journey."'

At Umarkot, he was taken to a bunker where a Brigadier and a few more senior officers interacted with him. The Brigadier reassuringly told him, 'You are now in safe hands and no harm will come to you!' Another senior officer asked Bhargav casually, 'Which part of India do you belong to?'

'Patiala, Punjab,' answered the young Pilot. There was a surprised gasp from the officer who responded rather jubilantly, 'Patiala! I too, am from Patiala! You must be knowing the famous cricket coach Baba Ram Kishan? I have learnt my cricket from him!'

It was Bhargava's turn to be surprised now. 'What a coincidence sir! I too have trained under him and played Ranji Trophy for Punjab under his guidance!'

With some sort of connection established, the Pakistani officers treated this POW fairly well that night and in the subsequent travels. 'I slept at the Dak Bungalow on a "Dunlop" mattress which gave some relief to my sore back! The next day, Captain Murtaza even lent me his shaving razor and soap cake so that I could look "officer like" again!'

Bhargava was now handed over to another agency who took him on his onward journey to Naya Chor in an open jeep, blindfolded. 'I realised that I was in a battle zone as I heard ack-ack firing, sound of fighter aircraft and arty shelling.'

Later, at a halt, they opened his blindfold inside a bunker. Another young-looking Brigadier introduced himself and questioned Bhargava over a cup of tea. 'I told him that my back pain was severe and I needed medical help as soon as possible.' The Brigadier obliged,

Author's Note: *I offered the Veteran to help write his biography and about his time in prison in Pakistan, I am sure that he has a whole stack of stories, ready for our consumption. Hopefully, I landed myself with another project, thanks to this story!*

SAVED BY A CHIT

LT GEN NARAYAN CHATTERJEE

Lieutenant General Narayan Chatterjee, PVSM, AVSM, SM, VSM, M-in-D[4] is a legendry flier of the erstwhile army Air Observation Post (AOP) flight of the artillery. Anyone who has studied a bit about Indian Army Aviation is sure to come across his name as one of the pioneers of aviation in the army—the man who was the force behind the formation of the Army Aviation Corps.

An alumnus of the Rashtriya Indian Military College (RIMC) and the National Defence Academy (NDA), 2nd Lt Chatterjee joined the elite 17 Para Field Regiment

4 Param Vishisht Seva Medal, Ati Vishisht Seva Medal, Sena Medal, Vishisht Seva Medal, Mentioned-in-dispatches

of the Artillery under the 50 Para Brigade of the Army located at Agra after graduating from the Indian Military Academy (IMA) in June, 1963.

'I was fortunate to get into this elite regiment. But to get accepted into the rank and file required extreme hard work. One had to prove himself mentally and physically robust to be the best of the best,' he tells me on a telephonic chat, adding that he was soon a 'Para Gunner'—a special breed of Artillery men who wore the maroon beret and could be dropped with their guns behind enemy lines to wreak havoc in the adversary's camp.

'It was early 1965, and war clouds loomed large. We were moved from Agra to the Raan of Kutch, which was the second flashpoint other than Kashmir—where the enemy was trying to fuel insurgency. Border skirmishes and firing on each other's patrols became a norm and as young officers, we got a taste of war early in our career.'

Chatterjee was the adjutant of the unit, right from the time it moved from Agra to the Rann. 'Mobilisation of such a large force needs planning, coordination and quick decision-making skills, something that I learnt on the job. Our seniors in the unit were legends and one could not dream of letting them down, especially in operations,' he reminisces.

The unit was moved during this 17-day war to the Lahore sector when the operations intensified and here, too, Chatterjee's unit played an active role in throwing back the intruding army. 'I still remember the areas of Biarbet, Dharamshala, sand-dunes and Point-84 which were prevented from falling into enemy hands, thanks to some good artillery bombardment followed by infantry operations,' he remembers.

Right from the day he became a para officer, Chatterjee had been exposed to aircraft, airmen, airfields and the medium of air. In his heart of hearts, he always dreamt of being in the cockpit, but being in the most elite, only para-artillery unit of the Indian Army, to voice this 'want' was difficult.

'My CO, Col RC Butalia during the war was also an AOP pilot and had motivated me to opt for flying. Whenever I saw AOP aircraft flying around in the forward area and directing the firing of our artillery guns, I wished I was up there doing the same!'

After the war, the unit moved back from Icchogil canal to Agra and then onward to the 'Sugar' sector, this time confronting the Chinese. 'It was good to be in the cool and serene hills of Himachal and, trips to Shimla were the most invigorating for us youngsters in those days!'

'My CO in the Sugar Sector was Col KK Hazari, (later VCOAS) who asked me one day if I wanted to opt for flying as an AOP pilot. My joy knew no bounds, I smiled ear to ear and said, "YES SIR!" immediately. I had just finished six years in uniform, and my life was going to take a new turn now.'

'Selected and found fit for flying, I went to fly the HT-2 at Bidar. I learnt my flying from Lt Vacha (Indian Navy) and Flt Lt PSI Iyengar who were my instructors. We also had Flt Lt's Beni, Rusty Kapoor, Sekhon and Bindra at Bidar, who became legends in the IAF and there was so much to learn from them.'

After, Bidar, Chatterjee went to Nasik to learn to fly the Krushak aircraft at the 665 AOP Squadron.

'Awarded with flying wings at Nasik, I was a double winger now! On my uniform, I proudly sported the para and the flying wings, something that very few in the Armed Forces wore in those times.' It was end of 1970 and he was posted to Jammu to the 661 AOP Squadron to fly the Auster Mk-IX which had recently replaced the ageing Mk-V.

'It was a versatile machine with the most reliable Bombardier "Cirrus" engine, and I was soon doing "shoots" with my fellow Artillery men at the ranges, enjoying every bit of time spent in the air. We had the best of IAF guys who maintained our machines and our bonhomie with the IAF mates at the Jammu airbase knew no bounds. I recall that my namesake was the Station Commander—a fine gentleman and a thorough professional.'

Within a few months, Chatterjee was fully operational and was soon to see another change in his aviation career. The Army was to get helicopters, and the first set of pilots were sent to the Helicopter Training School at Jodhpur to fly the Bell-47. 'To fly this helicopter, one had to get rid of many of the habits learnt while flying the fixed wing aircraft and I was soon comfortable in the noisy and vibrating environment of the helicopter.'

However, the conversion had to stop half way. War was imminent, all courses were cancelled and people sent back to their units to augment the manpower to fight. 'I was soon back at Jammu to fly the Auster Mk IX, and the training for war began in earnest.'

At that time, Chatterjee's unit had only two out of five aircrafts available for flying, the other three being unserviceable for want of spares. Two Pushpak aircraft were requisitioned from civil flying clubs for doing the tasks during the war.

'We soon had two Pushpaks and one Auster at Udhampur and two Auster's at Jammu. My aircraft at Jammu had the area of Chicken Neck, Chaamb, Marala Headworks to look after whilst the Udhampur guys looked after Akhnoor, Rajouri and Naushera sector.'

'We were op-ready all the time and the aircrafts were parked in camouflaged open pens near the runway at Jammu, always ready for take-off at short notice like they do in the Operational Readiness Platforms (ORPs) for fighters. Despite this, I found the time to go down to Udhampur to do a quick conversion on the Pushpak, so that I could fly it in operations should the need arise.'

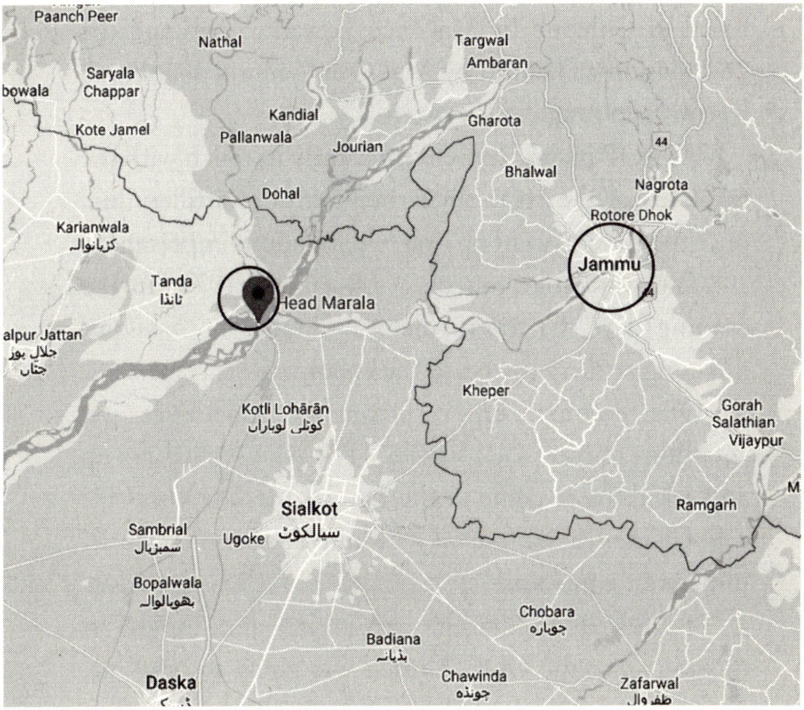

The location of the top secret mission.

'As a young captain, I was now qualified on the HT-2, Krushak, Auster, Bell-47 and the Pushpak! Not a mean feat at all!'

At that time, the 15 Corps based at Udhampur was commanded by Lt Gen Sartaj Singh, the 10 Division based in Chhamb by Maj Gen Jaswant Singh and the 26 Division at Jammu by Maj Gen Zorawar Bakshi, all legends and tough task masters.

'As AOP pilots, we were constantly in touch with the top brass of the HQ's since the control of artillery fire, once the balloon went up, was of paramount importance.'

The war broke out on 3 December, 1971. In the ensuing days, Chatterjee flew a number of missions, directing artillery fire on to the enemy.

One evening, on 9 December, Chatterjee got summons to meet Gen Bakshi. 'The ADC called me up and asked me to come to the Div HQ at 2030 hrs.' He told Chatterjee that the GOC wanted to personally brief him about a mission.

'I understood that it was a vital and top secret mission since the GOC himself was going to brief me. I set course in my Jeep along with my driver and escort and reached the Div HQ only to realise that the HQ had been shifted into operational shelters and located away from its permanent location in temporary sheds.'

'At the camping ground, the GOC awaited my arrival and I was soon ushered into his caravan along with one

Lt Col Narhari, (Later Lt Gen) who was the CO of the Engineer Regiment. Seeing Bakshi up close for the first time was intimidating for me as a young officer, but the General soon had both of us at ease.'

'He began, "This is a top-secret mission being monitored at the highest level. My young son, I want you take Narhari up with you tomorrow morning and fly towards the Marala Headworks. Use the camera of your aircraft and get me some good pictures as we want to assess the structure of the dam, thickness of the concrete and all relevant details that you can get us. Narhari, will carry a Rolleiflex camera and do some 'shooting' from the cockpit."'

'He continued, "I want you to get airborne as early as you can and I do not want you to discuss the mission with anyone. And yes, do not fly too close to the dam or cross over, we have intelligence inputs that the Pakistanis have fortified the areas around the dam. You might face some flak from them but I want you to be safe and get me the information which is most vital."'

Both the officers were now offered coffee by the General and as they departed, he slapped them on their backs and said, 'God Bless You Both!'

An excited Chatterjee was soon back at the airfield, getting his airmen to prepare the aircraft and informing the operations and ATC of his pre-dawn take-off, not disclosing where he was going.

'This was going to be a different operational mission, and I did not want any last minute delays or any untoward incident. We had excellent airmen, I remember their names today too. Corporal Rajkumar and one Sergeant Kumar were at the aircraft doing their checks on the machine in the darkness when I reached the tarmac in the morning. Believe me, Nitin, 30 to 40 years working alongside the IAF, flying all over the country, these airmen never let us down. The unity in the uniforms was unparalleled.'

My heart swelled up with pride when I heard these words about my service from the Army veteran.

It was a long sortie flown at low levels and they got what was required. They could also make note of the Pakistani deployment near the dam for information of the Indian forces.

'As we headed back, we were spotted by a MiG-19 that tried to follow us. I ducked down to tree-top heights and zigged zagged my way back to the airfield and I think the MiG lost me in the backdrop of the foliage, thankfully!'

The mission was a success. As they got down from the aircraft, the ATC officer, airmen and Jawans came running on the tarmac to receive them with handshakes. 'The hugs and slaps on our back we got that day can never be erased from memory,' says the ace.

'Marala Headworks was an important and strategic target for us. If we attacked the dam and caused sufficient damage, the gushing waters would cause flooding in the plains of Pakistan-Punjab wreaking havoc, and also not allowing movement of their armoured vehicles, should they try to enter our territory along the Punjab border.'

The dam, however, was not targeted as the war came to an end in 13 days. Till today, it is considered to be a strategic target. I personally think that if we destroy the dam, many civilians will die and many others will lose their livelihood.

Lt General Narayan Chatterjee has an amazing memory and can recount aircraft registration numbers, names of his ground crew as well as the names of places as he narrates stories from the war.

A memory he shared was his contribution to the counter attack on the advancing Pakistani forces in the Battle of Chhamb on the river Munnawar Tawi.

The GHQ orders to the GOC 23 Div, Gen Iftikhar of the Pakistan Army, were to clear the Indian held territory up to the river Munnawar Tawi. The General, in his wisdom, decided to attack from the hilly north side where movement of his armour was difficult. According to experts, his decision to do so was primarily to achieve surprise and also due to the fact that the Indians held the territory to the south much more strongly.

His plan was to reach the Mandiala bridge across the Tawi so as to force the Indians to withdraw from areas west of the river.

Although the Pakis achieved a fair degree of success in this operation, their plan was marred by the fact that their armour movement was restricted in narrow corridors. Furthermore, their logistic support was poor too. This led to a pause in the battle—a situation that allowed the Indians to re-organise themselves for a counter attack to throw the Pakistani forces out of the area.

'The counter attack on the Pakistani held positions on the banks of the Tawi was to be preceded by heavy artillery shelling to "soften" them up. That is where I came in. I think it was 10 December, 1971.'

'The Auster operating from Rakhmuti ALG which looked after the Chhamb sector became unserviceable. I got a call to reach Rakhmuti around 2 pm just after I had finished my lunch. There was a requirement to take a "shoot" in the evening and I was quite looking forward to it!'

His briefing went something like this:

*Heavy concentration of armour seen on the western bank of the Tawi in General area Chhamb. Armour likely to cross the Tawi with field artillery support at night. All fire units (Guns) of 10 and 26 Arty brigades available. Likely time for counter attack 1700, to end by last light. 26 Brigade Fire Direction Centre (FDC) will coordinate and control fire for both brigades. Radio frequency ****. Contact on getting airborne for further information.*

Happy Shooting!

Major Anand, (he still remembers!) was the Brigade Major (BM) of 26 Brigade who had briefed Chatterjee that afternoon. The GOC 15 Corps as well as 10 Division Commander were in the general area controlling the counter attack. It was important that the Pakistanis be beaten back now, otherwise we would lose Chammb sector, may be forever, or the Pakistanis would use these gains as a bargaining power at the end of the hostilities.

'The sun was in the west, directly into my eyes and I could not see much except for the dust kicked up by the tanks. I knew where to direct the fire and went up on radio.'

'Six for all stations, over!'

'Six for all stations over...confirm ready...'

No reply. It was exasperating. 'I wondered if I had selected the wrong frequency or there was some botch up in the communication with the formations. An idea struck me as I was re-tuning my radio set to try the communication again. I had a small bag which was used to drop important mail over posts. I scribbled down the frequency on a piece of paper, put it in the bag and flew low to drop it at the gun area of the 10 arty brigade!'

After a few seconds, the FDC came up loud and clear!

'Hello 6! Guns ready to fire! Over!' Chatterjee heaved a sigh of relief and his adrenalin kicked in.

'I rechecked with the FDC if all guns were available since we needed the full volume of fire on to the target.'

'All available for 6! Over and out!' came the reply.

'I, thereafter, directed the fire of 104 guns of the artillery on to the target. The simultaneous fire from so many guns rained down on the enemy and pulverised them, a sight I can never forget till my last breath.'

'Hello 6 from Big tiger,' crackled the radio set. 'Targets neutralised, excellent shooting! My compliments! Return to base safely. Over and out!' Big Tiger was the GOC complimenting the brave Chatterjee on his role during the bombardment.

The Pakistani assault on Chhamb had been averted, but the forces on ground needed to get hold of the western bank of the Tawi, as part of the counter-attack plan. Through the night of 10 December, after some fierce fighting, the western bank of the river was again occupied by our forces.

An elated Chatterjee flew back to the airfield in the dying moments of the day.

The light was fading and he was low on fuel again. 'I decided to land at Jammu which had some night landing facilities and ATC. I remember that my friend Flight Lieutenant GD Trivedi was on radio that evening.'

'As I was flying from the border area near Akhnoor, I was spotted again by a MiG-19, but this time he too was in a hurry to get back to his base and left me alone. I flew to Jammu at tree top level.'

Another surprise awaited Chatterjee as he came in

for landing at Jammu. The runway was blocked from both ends by concrete filled barrels and landing wasn't possible. 'I was the only aircraft flying in their area and once I announced my predicament over the radio, the ATC was quick to react. DSC Jawans, Airmen and my own troops got together and moved the obstructions within the time I got to do one orbit over the airfield, yet again displaying the true spirit of jointmanship.'

While he did his mission, intelligence reports had come in that the Pakistanis were going to try and land or para-drop their troops to take over the airfield at Jammu. To thwart their intent, the station commander had ordered that the runway be made un-operational by placing the obstructions. 'In fading light, I landed with the red low level warning light for fuel yet again!'

'Just think of it, my mission would have failed if I hadn't hit upon the idea of dropping the bag with the piece of paper over the FDC. Who knows, the war would have taken a different turn, maybe!'

I realised that our conversation had been going on for an hour while I took down notes. I asked the valiant soldier to narrate one more anecdote before we disconnected.

'Yes, during the war, my Auster finished its flying hours and was due for major overhaul at the Base Repair Depot (BRD). We needed a change of aircraft and I was told to ferry the aircraft to 2 BRD at Gwalior and get back a new one.'

'The station commander insisted that I take a navigator along so that he would be of some help in the cockpit. He told me that air raids were imminent at the intermediate airfields of Chandigarh and Palam and there was a good chance of diverting to other airfields.'

'Take Flt Lt Mishra with you, he is an excellent Nav,' said the Commander.

It was Mishra who accompanied Chatterjee on his ferry to Gwalior the next day. He had all his maps and navigation paraphernalia along and was comfortable flying in the cockpit of the Auster.

'As the Commander had predicted, some miles inbound to Chandigarh, the ATC informed me that an air raid was imminent at the base and I was to divert to either Patiala or Ambala.'

Mishra was quick to react, he quickly calculated the navigation parameters and told Chatterjee, 'Steer course*** degrees and apply an offset of 10 degrees for winds from the left......we should be overhead Patiala in 27 minutes...'

'Flying at roof-top level, we reached bang over Patiala and executed a safe landing, thanks to a very professional Mishra!' After the air raid alert was over, they went on with their ferry to Gwalior and handed over the aircraft for servicing at the BRD.

'Alas, the BRD had no new aircraft to offer us and therefore, without wasting time, we flew back to Jammu in a transport aircraft the same day, to get back to participate in the war.'

Lieutenant General Narayan Chatterjee retired from the army in 2003. Prior to hanging his uniform, he was one of the core group of officers deputed to formulate the Joint Implementation Directive 1986, which led to the formation of the Army Aviation Corps. He has logged more than 5,500 hours of accident and incident-free flying in his long aviation career and has taken part in operations in the Siachen as well as in Sri Lanka.

He has also represented India in World Helicopter Symposium organised by the American Helicopter Society in Norfolk, Virginia, in 1997, and has been actively associated with the Hindustan Aeronautics Limited (HAL) for retro-fitment of Chetak and Cheetah, and development of the Advanced Light Helicopter (ALH) from its inception. He has travelled to many countries to study the concept of employment of the Army Aviation Corps.

The decorated veteran pilot is a soldier and an aviation enthusiast to the core, and his talks at various aviation-related gatherings are anecdotal and always a pleasure to hear. As he hung up, he promised me that he would narrate me another interesting story of how the Army Aviation Corps came into being at a later date.

I look forward to that day.

SECTION TWO

THE KARGIL WAR

INTRODUCTION

1999

MORE THAN two and a half decades had passed since we had taken part in a full-fledged war since 1971. What we had seen in this period was an increase in the intensity of militancy, especially in Jammu and Kashmir, and this had kept our Armed Forces busy. Soldiers had to now learn to fight in built up terrain, fight intense short skirmishes in the jungles where guerrilla warfare ruled the roost, and we also had to carry out what is popularly known as WHAM (Winning Hearts And Minds) operations.

Winning the hearts and minds of the people of Jammu and Kashmir, though a daunting task, had been well-received and benefitted a large population of the strife-torn state. Bad politics surviving on religious sentiments, as well as interference from our neighbours set us back, little by little, on whatever progress was being made in this area.

The Pakistani machinery, be it at the political or military level, continued its efforts of making India 'bleed by a thousand cuts' to take revenge for what we did to their country in 1971. In fact, some historians believe that for Pakistan's survival as a nation state, an anti-India tirade is a necessity. Advocating the same belief, no efforts had been spared by Pakistan to support Muslim sentiments and fan trouble in the Kashmir Valley.

Emboldened by some successes but also some setbacks by some Indian efforts at containing militancy in 1998, Pakistan decided to do something more solid and dramatic on their part to cause grievous hurt to our nation.

As part of an unwritten agreement between the two militaries, troops from both sides vacated posts held at high altitudes during winters, mainly for administrative purposes. It was barely liveable at those altitudes and super low temperatures. The heavy snow made it a difficult terrain for movement on either side. The summers, naturally, saw both sides come face to face at these posts.

In the winter of 1998, the Pakistani military took advantage of this unwritten pact and with the help of the Mujahedeen, Pak army regulars were sent in to take over the Indian posts with an aim to re-align the 'Line of Control.' The advantage of this occupation of Indian posts was huge for Pakistan.

Firstly, they now had a bird's-eye view of the Dras-Kargil-Batalik area and could monitor Indian troop movements on the only road leading from Srinagar to Leh.

Secondly, they could direct accurate artillery fire on to the road or any other targets which were now in their field of view whenever they wanted to.

Thirdly, by squeezing the Srinagar-Leh road artery, they could choke vehicular movement to the Siachen Glacier, thereby, throttling and weakening the Indian stance in that area held since 1984.

Last but not the least, by occupying these posts and not giving them back, the Pakis would deal a blow to the morale of the Indian Army, and India as a whole.

Despite the fact that some inputs of the Pakistani ingress were available to the Indian side, the first part of the infiltration plan was a success. The Pakistani troops dug in, made our bunkers their new home and established the logistic lines of support to improve their sustenance and sustainability through the harsh winters. Blame it on intelligence failure or a lackadaisical approach by the Indian side, to evict the Pakistanis from well dug-in fortified bunkers was going to be difficult. But this had to be done and it was going to be tough, really tough.

And that is what happened. When the enormity of the situation dawned, and Indian troops were rushed in for operations, it was realised that the combat power required to push the intruders back would require ratios of almost 12-15 to 1. That is, for every one Pak soldier sitting in the fortified bunker, 12 to 15 Indian soldiers were needed. Moreover, large casualties were to be expected on the Indian side in such a scenario.

It was literally and figuratively an uphill battle for our brave soldiers to do what they did in the next eight weeks or so. Operation 'Vijay' for the army and 'Safed Sagar' for the air force was finally declared closed by Prime Minister Atal Bihari Vajpayee on 26 July 1999, telling the world that the Pakistani intruders had been finally evicted from Indian territory.

This defeat for the Pakistanis and the win for India came at a humungous loss. As per official figures, 527 Indian soldiers were killed, three times that injured, and three aircraft were lost. The Pakistani losses, as claimed by us, include about 700 plus killed, and a 1,000 plus injured.

This was the first time Indians saw the war unfolding —sitting in their bedrooms—primarily due to the free hand given to the media. When the guns fell silent and the statisticians and historians got down to researching their stories, the soldiers who fought the war slowly disappeared into oblivion...

2022

But these men and women, who had seen things closely and upfront, were in the know of intimate details of what happened—stories which had not yet been brought out into the open. If not now, these stories would fade from memory soon, and be lost for ever.

That's where I come in. In a bid to get some 'oral history,' I went around speaking to a large number of soldiers, both retired and serving, and found out snippets of information from which I wove stories that brought out the human and humane aspects of the war.

This section is my attempt to show the readers—Kargil from the skies.

So, sit alongside those wonderfully brave soldiers in their flying machines and go for a sortie to understand the Kargil conflict from a different perspective…

THE SNOW AND THE SHRAPNEL

COL GAUTAM KHOT

Born on 18 October 1967 at Pune in a middle class family, Colonel Gautam Khot joined the National Defence Academy in June, 1984 after his schooling in Mumbai as an army cadet. Ever since childhood, he dreamt of flying. He joined the Air Defence Artillery and later opted for army aviation in 1993, going on to became a helicopter pilot a year later.

He flew extensively during his flying tenure in all parts of the country and amassed 4,000 hours of flying experience on the Chetak and Cheetah helicopters including flying in the higher reaches of the Himalayas. In 1999, he flew many missions in the Kargil conflict for which he earned himself a Vir Chakra for gallantry.

The veteran, now settled in Pune, sought premature retirement from the army after serving for 22 years and now flies helicopters in the corporate sector.

This is his story.

Colonel Gautam Khot had just been posted at the Army Aviation Unit at Bareilly from the 'valley' (Srinagar-Jammu and Kashmir) where he had spent an exciting operational tenure of three years. He was now enjoying peace and tranquil at this quiet station where flying involved going to the three beautiful valleys of Harsil-Gangotri, Joshimath-Badrinath, and Pithoragarh in the mountains of erstwhile western Uttar Pradesh, now Uttarakhand. At 32, he had just found some quality time to spend with family and he was getting used to being with his children—a daughter, 4 year-old and a son, just a toddler.

He remembers the date clearly. 'It was 3 June 1999 when we received orders to upstick from Bareilly and move to Srinagar the very next day. We were to be based at the army aviation base at Shariffabad near Srinagar. I was quite comfortable going—having had bags of experience in that area in my previous tenure. Therefore, I took it upon myself to train the other pilots who were new to the area.'

'Very soon, I was redeployed as a detachment commander at Sonamarg from where I operated for the rest of the period in question.'

Gautam remembers that there was a mammoth movement of men and material on the road to Dras, and the job of the army aviation units in the area was to assist in getting men, material, food, weapons and clothing to areas not connected by roads. This would help the troops settle down into their bunkers the soonest. During the operations that followed, these helicopters were very helpful in saving many lives of critically injured soldiers. Gautam himself evacuated about 65 injured soldiers to safety in the time he flew during the conflict.

The unit was equipped with the Cheetah helicopter which had limited volume and therefore, weight carrying capacity. The heavier weights were being carried by the Mi-17s but those were limited in number and were given tasks in order of priority and importance.

'In the six weeks of intense operations, I flew more than 110 hours! Often, we landed at unprepared landing sites which were hastily created helipads just a few metres in length and breadth, barely able to accommodate our helicopter. As we went in for landing, we were often greeted with arty shelling by the enemy.'

We discussed various aspects of aviating in such conditions, and I sought answers from him to my many questions. 'What was the flying environment like? What were some of the memorable sorties that you were a part of? How was the morale of your boys and the troops?'

At that time, I was posted at a forward base in

Rajasthan, flying the Mi-35 attack helicopter. The days were tense and the conflict was threatening to escalate to a full-fledged war along the front which we guarded. Missions were planned and our firing skills were honed so that we could deliver our weapons on target when the time came. Unfortunately, this did not happen. Our aircraft was a potent weapon platform, but wasn't designed to operate at the altitudes of Kargil. While we prepared for war, we felt sorry that we could not go in support of our brethren who flew the not so potent Mi-17s and the smaller machines up north. If we had been able to go there, we would have pulverized the enemy positions with our firepower! Sitting amidst the hot sands of the desert, we had to make do with only the news of what was happening at Srinagar and beyond. I told Gautam how I wished I was there with him during the conflict as I went through a rewind. 'I can remember each day of the operations as if it happened yesterday,' he told me.

'Tololing was captured on 18 June. Our boys had pushed the Pakis back by almost 200-300 metres from the top. There were remnants of resistance from the retreating soldiers and sporadic firing could be heard. On the morning of 19 June, barely a few hours from cessation of the fight for capture of the all-important peak, my helicopter and I were right there. Smoke still emanated from the hillside blocked from our view. The helipad—a cleared piece of flat ground barely 2 by 2 metres, located out of sight of the enemy was just large enough to take the skis[5] of my helicopter.'

'We had taken off from Dras helipad with an important consignment of drinking water. I was told that the troops had radioed for water as an immediate emergency requirement. They must have been really thirsty after a rough night of fighting with bullets flying all around. I was aware that they would have eaten snow to keep their parched throats lubricated, further aggravating their hunger for water.'

The helipad was barely a couple of kilometres away but it involved rapid climb to 15,000 odd feet. That was quite telling on the machine which was loaded to the hilt and the pilots flying were, as usual, gasping for oxygen in the rarefied atmosphere.[6]

'While approaching for landing at the so-called helipad, we were in view of the enemy and shelling and firing commenced as soon as they heard us descend to land. The Pakistanis weren't so lucky and God was on our side. Soon, the soldiers were happy to have a few hundred litres of water to drink. On the return leg, we picked up two critically injured soldiers and got them to

---

5 Skis are fitted on the helicopter to facilitate it to land in soft snow.
6 Helicopter cockpit of the machines which flew in Kargil were unpressurised and pilots needed to breathe oxygen from portable cylinders carried on board.

the hospital at Dras. Doctors at the field hospital at Dras were working round the clock trying to save the lives of casualties arriving by the dozens.'

'That day, I flew six missions to the posts around Tololing giving them water and food and evacuating back casualties to the hospital. It left me physically and emotionally drained.'

'Another sortie I remember was when we were tasked to lift artillery ammunition to a gun area where vehicles could not reach due to enemy shelling. It was a massive three tonnes of effort,[7] and we had to cart it up 200 kg at a time. With this, we ensured that our guns never fell silent for lack of ammunition, and also helped to neutralise whatever little resistance being offered by the defeated troops of the Pakistani Army. At all times during the mission, we saw tracers flying at us, but we flew undeterred.'

'On one of the approaches to land at a forward helipad called Parion ka Talab, we saw artillery shells landing right on the helipad. Dark holes appeared in the snow as the shells went in. And then they exploded, showering snow high up in the air, the shock waves juddering the helicopter and us too. Due to the snow, we were saved being hit by shrapnel. We aborted the mission and returned later.'

---

7 The total weight of the ammunition that was carried to the artillery gun post.

'In another mission, two helicopters dropped 12 men, one man at a time, to an unoccupied post in Mushko valley at 17,000 feet. Had this mission failed, the enemy would have certainly moved in and occupied it,' reminisces the gallant veteran.

For his act of bravery in the face of the enemy, Col Gautam Khot was awarded the Vir Chakra, the medal and citation proudly displayed at his home. He also has been felicitated by the Maharashtra Government for this act of valour.

'What was the first reaction when you went into the war?' I ask the veteran before we say our good-byes.

'When I landed at Sonamarg and saw the intimidating snow-capped mountains all around, the tops of which the enemy had occupied, I wondered how our army was going to fight from this position of disadvantage. But fight we did... and won! As I look back, I do feel that it should have escalated to a full-fledged war. We could have sorted them out once and for all!'

INTELLIGENT JAGUARS

GROUP CAPTAIN
ASHWANI BHAKOO

Psychotherapist, Aviation Consultant, MSc (Strategy & Leadership), MS (Psychotherapy & Counselling), PGDPC, MMS, Certified for Science of Happiness & Happiness at Work, Qualified Flying Instructor, Pilot Attack Instructor

GP CAPT ASHWANI BHAKOO

That is what Group Captain Ashwani Bhakoo's visiting card reads today. He is a decorated ex-fighter pilot of the IAF who mainly flew the Jaguar Deep Penetration Strike Aircraft (DPSA) in his career spanning almost 25 years. He was the commanding officer of a frontline Jaguar squadron during the Kargil Conflict in which his unit boys earned seven gallantry awards.

My earliest memories of Group Capt Ashwani Bhakoo are of the Gorakhpur days. He was posted as the Station Flight Safety and Investigation Officer (SFS&IO) and was known to be a hard task master. I was in Gorakhpur, practising leading a six-helicopter formation flypast for a colour presentation ceremony. The President of India was to award Presidential Colours to 17 Squadron located at Gorakhpur itself and the 114 Helicopter Unit, located at Leh.

It was a matter of honour for all to see that the show went off flawlessly. While I led the six helicopters, Bhakoo sir sat atop the ATC and controlled the fighter and helicopter formations, ensuring that we were always bang on time and over 'target'—passing over the dais as the parade commander presented the salute to the Supreme Commander.

In 1999, Bhakoo was the Commanding Officer of 14 Squadron flying the Jaguars. The role of the squadron was to carry out bombing and photo recce missions. I asked him to narrate his experiences of the war.

'My squadron was located at Ambala and due to the good range of our aircraft, we could fly into the war zone and come back to base after the missions. I was the leader in many of them, and we were spearheading the Intelligence Gathering[8] efforts to determine the positions of enemy infiltrators in the Dras-Kargil axis.'

8 Intelligence gathering is of vital importance for conduct of successful operations. These are done before, during and even after cessation of the operations.

'The Pakistani troops had infiltrated, aided by the Mujahedeen and other terrorist groups into our territory and had taken up vantage positions. They were now overlooking the road to Dras and could play merry hell into our logistics chain whenever they wanted to. Whether it was intelligence failure or not, is another point of discussion and I won't go into that. But the fact of the matter is that the Army thought that it was a minor incursion and therefore did not ask the air force to check on what was the actual position on the ground.'

'When things got a little hot and the confusion started clearing, the army finally asked for a recce mission which was flown by a Canberra aircraft piloted by late Wing Commander Perumal Alagharaja. (Perumal, or Peru as he was popularly known, retired as a Group Captain and flew for a commercial airline. He, unfortunately, passed away in January 2012 of a heart attack.)

During this sortie, Perumal's Canberra was hit by a stinger missile and lost power on one of its engines. The brave Peru nursed his aircraft back to Srinagar without any instruments to carry out a safe landing, and was awarded a Shaurya Chakra for the same. He made history by being the first IAF fighter plane to have returned home after a missile hit.

'What this incident told us is that the Pakistanis were on the hilltops in good numbers and they were definitely not the Mujahids or terrorists as claimed initially. They were trained soldiers who held state-of-the-art anti-aircraft missiles to shoot down our airplanes.

'We were in business well before the actual operations had started. In fact, without our recce missions, further operations could not be planned at all—so important was the requirement.'

'The squadron was given very little time to prepare for the recce missions which were to fly from Ambala and take photos of the area along the LOC in the Srinagar valley. The photo films were to be analysed immediately and the report rendered to the commanders and decision-makers at the Army and Air HQ.'

'Hitherto, some of the sorties had been flown by Mig-21s with photo pods and the results were not encouraging. Later, the MiG-21s also tried an innovative method of filming with a portable video camera being carried in a trainer aircraft (which had two pilots) on a mission. With this better resolution filming, preliminary analysis suggested that the enemy was present in big numbers at various points along the LOC.'

'So, we decided to fly low, in a formation of four. We were equipped with some self-defence equipment like the "Chaff" and "Flares" (which can fool radar controlled or heat seeking missiles) and some rounds of front guns for self-defence. We did the complete run from Srinagar to the Siachen, maintaining radio silence and being escorted by the potent MiG-29 as Air Defence escorts. We flew pretty low, sometimes at just about 400 feet above the crest line, and at the end of the mission, we had captured enough evidence for planning the future action.'

'In all our missions after this one, we had a threat of the F-16s, the frontline fighter aircraft of the Pakistan Air Force (PAF), who, we were aware, were being scrambled from across. But our MiG-29s were good enough to ward them off and we were able to do our missions unhindered. Right through the Kargil conflict, we flew these missions and got valuable information for our other strike force missions to go through with pin-point accuracy.'

'The squadron flew more than 50 to 60 missions during the conflict and continued to do so even after the guns fell silent in July end 1999. 'Our information on the enemy positions was important to our artillery Bofors guns too, who, with this data, were able to deliver devastating attacks on enemy gun positions and other targets,' says the veteran. 'We had special photo recce pods which could look deep inside enemy territory even while maintaining the sanctity of the border as we were ordered to do.'

The IAF had clear orders not to violate the LOC because the leadership felt that it would lead to escalation of the conflict. The missions were flown at low and high levels depending on the level of clarity and details required from the aerial photography.

'My boys in the squadron were so full of josh. Pilots

had been augmented from their staff duties to the squadron to make up for numbers. There used to be a huge tussle amongst all of them to get their names on the missions!'

The engineering and administrative staff of the squadron were not to be left behind. Tents were deployed inside the squadron complex and the men refused to go home even for their meals. 'All that was left for me to do was to plan the missions in consultation with Western Air Command.'

'When I asked the men how they were going to manage the food, water and ration requirements while staying inside the technical area, they replied, "Sir, you do the missions, and leave the rest to us. We will manage everything else on ground!"'

The veteran today is settled in Pune and dabbles in a lot of social work and delivers lectures in schools, colleges, and institutions of repute. 'My retired Jaguar aeroplane now operates within a radius of 500 km from Pune!' he says with a chuckle.

HERNIATED DISC AND LASER GUIDED BOMBS

GROUP CAPTAIN AJAY DEVIDAS PURANDHARE

Veteran Group Captain Ajay Devidas Purandhare left the IAF after 25 years of glorious service in 2016. He believes in working silently, and therefore, it was quite a task to get him to speak about his experiences of Kargil. But speak he did and brought out a plethora of issues around which I knit this story.

Gp Capt Ajay has flown the MiG-21 and the Mirage 2000 aircraft. He has also had the opportunity to have a taste of flying the helicopters when he was posted as a directing staff at the prestigious Tactics and Air Combat Development Establishment (TACDE). TACDE is the institution where the top-gun pilots of the IAF ideate and create new tactics to be used by IAF aircraft in their operational and offensive roles. To get to do a course at this establishment, only the best men are selected, and to become an instructor here, obviously, the best of those best. You can very well imagine how competent one needs to be to get there as Purandhare did.

Ajay has tonnes of experience on the Mirage 2000 aircraft, which we will call M2K in short. He was posted at the elite No 1 Squadron at Gwalior during the Kargil ops. Having had a spinal injury which kept him grounded for two years, the young man was just finding his feet in the squadron in 1999. 'I still had a few niggles in my back which required rest and looking after, off and on, and thankfully, my squadron bosses were very kind to keep me off flying.'

'I was made the Adjutant of the squadron during that time and my job involved looking after the men and their administrative requirements as well as handling all the non-operational paperwork of the squadron. This experience was going to prove very vital for me as we were sucked into the battle in the heights of Kargil.'

'At 0330 hours on 26 May, 1999, I got a call from my flight commander asking me if I was fit enough to take on a mission.' Realising that something serious was brewing, and the fact that his flight commander wouldn't have called him at this unearthly hour, his response was immediate, 'I am always ready, Sir!'

'As I stepped out into the darkness with a hurriedly packed bag, my wife asked me the usual, "When will you be back?"'

'In a couple of days was the simplest answer I could think of. I didn't know I would be proved very wrong (like many other times) this time. I actually set foot back in my home base after three months!'

The M2K was ordered by India in 1982 as a counter to the purchase of Lockheed Martin F-16s by Pakistan from the US around the same time. The state-of-the-art aircraft, total 36 in number, arrived in India in 1985 and were soon operational in two squadrons—No 1 and No 7 based at Gwalior. The aircraft was designed in the 1970s and has served the western forces very well over the years. Dassault Aviation, which manufactures the aircraft, has continued to modify and upgrade its systems and the latest upgrade would keep the aircraft fit for fighting beyond 2030. It was one of the fastest fighter aircraft on inventory at that time with a top speed of 2,400 kmph (2.2 mach) and a good range of 1,500 km. With time, the IAF has added a few more of these to its inventory.

A very versatile machine with the best electronics and weapons, the M2K has served us very well even in the recent strikes at Balakot and also did yeoman service in the Kargil war. In the Kargil war, the IAF realised how potent a weapon platform it was. Naturally so, the IAF looked at its big brother, the Rafale, as the next machine of choice to succeed this generation of fighters for enhancing its combat potential.

Back to the story, Ajay, slightly uncomfortable with his back condition, but keen on doing the mission, was airborne with full load as the sun went up and landed at a forward base by 0545. He was immediately briefed for his next mission—to escort a MiG-25 on a photo reconnaissance mission over the enemy territory. The story of the unique MiG-25 mission is narrated in another chapter in this book.

'This was the first time that we all were exposed to high altitude missions and we were overawed by the scenic beauty that the mighty Himalayas had on offer. It was also another experience to manoeuvre a fully-loaded aircraft at that altitude—these were challenging missions and the threat of enemy air action loomed large,' says Ajay.

As the adjutant of his squadron, his duties also included looking after the administrative arrangements at the new base for his men so that they were comfortable at their workplace.

'There was really no time to think—missions after missions were to be flown and my motivated men did a superb job in keeping the planes in good nick round the clock.' Besides some offensive task at the later stage of the conflict, the M2Ks were initially used for escort to strike missions, ELINT (Electronic Intelligence), and to carry out CAP (Combat Air Patrol)[9] over designated areas. The body and mind took a lot of beating but we were young then and could hack it,' says the veteran who manages his own software company now at Vadodara in Gujarat.

'We were already trained for long duration missions before this conflict. So, three missions per day was a norm and we did them happily. The aircraft had very good automated systems and high-end technology to ease cockpit and pilot workload. Therefore, a lot of flying to and from the target area was left to the autopilot which helped us to be relaxed when it was actually required.'

'Bombing from high altitudes with dumb weapons[10] like 500 kg bombs is highly inaccurate due to a number of factors. If you miss by a couple of meters, the bomb either falls miles away into the ravine or crevasse and loses its effectiveness. That was what was happening to the bombs dropped from the MiG-23/27 fleet and therefore a need was felt to employ precision weapons for these bunkers and tents perched on mountain tops,' narrates the veteran.

---

9 Combat air patrol is carried over own territory to ensure that the enemy fighters do not interfere with our missions. They also are a show of force, warning the enemy to lay off.

10 A dumb bomb is a dead weight which, when dropped from an aircraft falls to ground aided by gravity. Therefore, once dropped the weapon cannot be controlled. In contrast, the bombs which have laser guidance or any other form of control can be 'guided' on to the target and are, therefore, called Precision bombs.

'Precision weapons require precise electronic equipment and guidance which the M2K was built for, and therefore, despite the high cost of the weapon, it was decided to use the Laser Guided Bombs (LGBs) to take out the targets which posed the gravest danger to us in their order of priority.

Another thing that our brave technicians did was to modify the normal bombs to laser guided ones. This was done by strapping on a special kit to these bombs so that they behaved like the accurate laser guided ones and did not miss the target. What was amazing about this modification was that it was done in record time by various agencies of R&D and the test pilots at Aircraft Systems Testing Establishment (ASTE) based at Bangalore. This modification, some experts opine, led to early degradation of the enemy positions and brought an end to the conflict.

'It was almost August when I came back to base after an adventure of a lifetime that I can never erase from memory. As soon as I kept my bags down, it was time to visit the doctor again. I had a prolapsed disc with all the flying and hardships my body had endured, and had to be admitted at the Base Hospital in Delhi. There, I met with many a wounded soldier, including some of my NDA friends who recuperated alongside me. I understood how different and a bloody battle the men on the ground had fought.'

FIGHTING THE CROSS WINDS

AIR MARSHAL RAGHUNATH NAMBIAR

I heard of the story of the first drop of Laser Guided Bombs from Air Marshal Raghunath Nambiar, who was then a Wing Commander posted at Gwalior air base (which was home to the Mirages) looking after flight safety aspects.

Namby sir, as he is known in the IAF, was a very experienced pilot on the M2K with almost 2,000 hours on the aircraft. He had had the privilege to fly and test many other types of aeroplanes as an Experimental Test Pilot (ETP) while posted at the Aircraft Systems and Testing Establishment (ASTE). He was augmented to the 'Battle Axes' squadron for flying duties as soon as it moved to Adampur in Punjab for the operations.

'I had the target in sight, on my scope at almost 50 km well before we reached the weapon release line. We were firing at the six to seven white tents on Tiger Hill with one laser-guided bomb from each aircraft. But there was a problem. At 28,000 feet, we had a very strong component of cross-wind of almost 70 knots (130 kmph) which was likely to deviate the weapon from target. A quick decision was made, and we descended to 26,000 feet where the winds were within acceptable limits, and cruised in towards the target—all systems "On" for sending the bomb to its destination.'

'I pressed the trigger and the aircraft bucked like a horse, losing 600 kg of metal filled with explosives from under its belly. The bomb was on its way now and as I turned the aircraft away with my sights slaved to the target, I waited with bated breath watching the small screen in front of me. The 30 seconds of bomb flight seemed like eternity and then—whoosh! The entire screen went white showing the impact on the tents. The smoke and debris went high and obscured the target for a while. We were sure we had not missed the tents and elated after tasting first blood. It was hoped that our ground forces would now find it easy to mop up what was left of the enemy on tiger hill. A few days later, the news was confirmed. Tiger Hill had fallen.'

'The sortie planning for the mission had started on the evening of 22 June, when we received orders to attack enemy positions on Tiger Hill the next day. The target as shown in the photographs provided appeared to be 6 to 7 white tents on top of the hill. Take off was planned at 0630 hours from Adampur with escorts being provided by two more M2Ks from Ambala (From the "Tigers" Squadron). The rendezvous happened in the air as planned and all four aircrafts set course for the target.'

'Tiger Hill has a unique shape when seen in photographs. From the heights the M2Ks were flying, all the mountains merge into one big mass of jagged rocks with valleys appearing as dark lines. The only feature that stood out in this area was Mount Godwin Austen (Mt K2) which towered above this mass at 28,251 feet, just a couple of thousand feet below the height we had planned to fly.'

'We had the electronics in our aircraft which we were thankful for. Searching for the target in the jagged rocky mountains interspersed with snow with bare eyes was like searching for the proverbial needle in the haystack. Luckily, we had the technology to show us a clear picture of the seven tents on our scopes. It was very similar to the photos we were shown while we planned the mission.'

'As we closed in to firing distance, we realised that there was a small fuzz of a cloud covering the target area and "lasing" the target and thereafter guiding the bomb on the laser beam was not possible. Due to this constraint, they set up an orbit and conserved fuel to wait for this cloud to move out.'

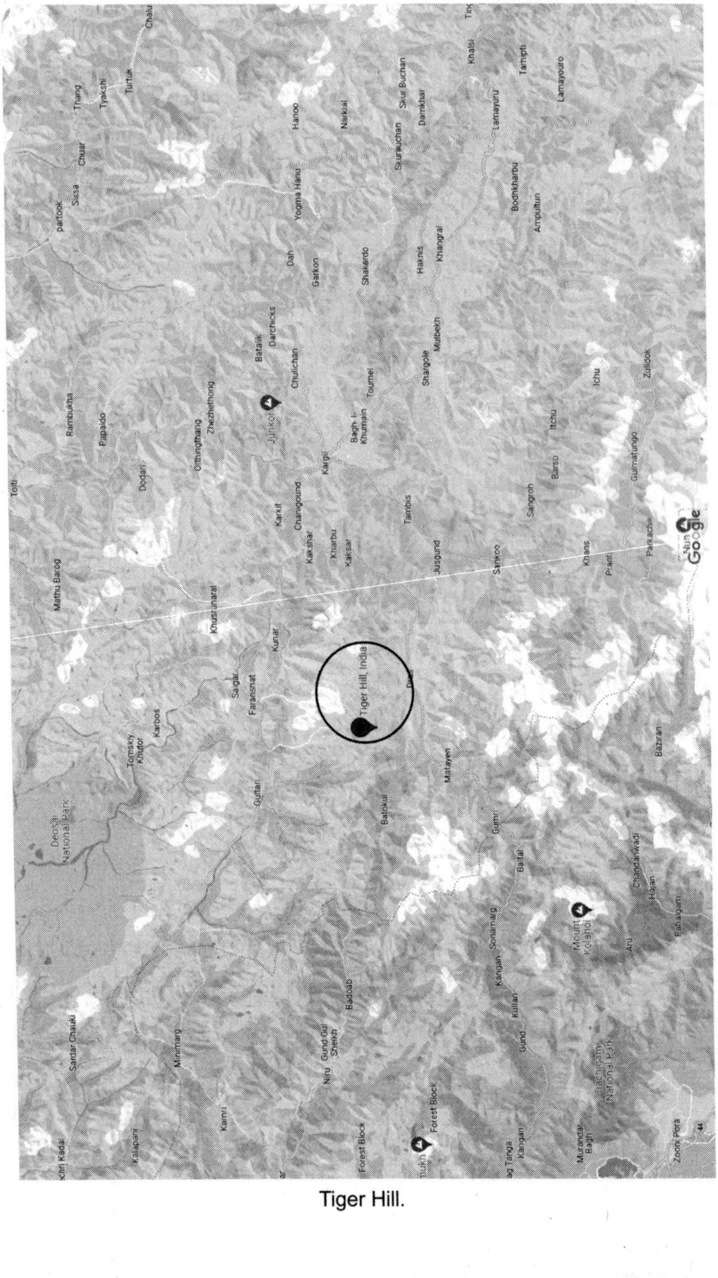
Tiger Hill, India
Deosai National Park
Kargil
Junkol
Mount Kolahoi
Drass
Google

Tiger Hill.

The luck was on the Pakistani side that morning. The cloud persisted and the aircraft had to return to base without letting go their weapons. The intruders were safe for another day on the hill. On the next day, three more attempts were made in the morning but were unsuccessful due to clouding over the target area.

'In the fourth attempt, as we turned away from the target, Monish (the pilot in the second aircraft) yelled at me, "Flare left" indicating a missile launch. I instantly throttled back to idle power and hauled the aircraft upward in a steep left turn and commenced dropping flares.[11] I did not spot the tiny shoulder launched missile,[12] but Monish did see it climb towards us, and thereafter, fall away as we were outside its envelope.'

The sortie was re-planned for the next day and the then Chief of the Air Staff, Air Chief Marshal AY Tipnis flew in to Adampur and decided to join in for the mission. A third fighter was planned in which the Chief flew in the rear seat to get a first-hand experience of the attack and conflict.

11 To ward of the missile threat, flares are fired from the aircraft which creates a false heat source that confuses the seeker head of the missile.

12 Shoulder launched missiles are man portable anti-aircraft missiles as the stinger in this case. They have shorter kill ranges and generally have heat seeking heads, implying that the missile locks on to the heat source of the aircraft—its exhaust.

As the bombs hit the target, they searched around the area looking for any more signs of the enemy. On the return leg, they flew over Tiger Hill at a lower height to film the destroyed target and assess the damage.

The smoke had cleared and nothing was left on top of the hill.

After landing at base, the photo films were analysed. The photos clearly showed four soldiers running inside the camp area just before the bomb impact.

ANECDOTES AND EXPERIENCES

Another pilot who flew in the mission and does not want to be named, told me that he was able to count as many as 16-18 missiles being fired upon the attacking formation that morning. That clearly shows the kind of arsenal the enemy had amassed, and their intentions too. Due to the attrition caused by our air force, the ground forces were quick to capitalise on the opportunity and were able to take back the heights of Tiger Hill, albeit after a bloody battle.

Munto Dhalo was an important logistics base for the Pakistani intruders. It had a road-head (roads leading close to their camp) and this made it easy for the enemy to stockpile their stores in large quantities. This base was used as a supply point to deliver rations, ammunition, and other war fighting wherewithal to the other bunkers at heights occupied in the area.

On our side, logistic management was a major issue. Men, material and every other war fighting equipment needed to be taken to the post by helicopter or by means of porters from where the road ended, a slow and tedious task. This also meant that replenishments during contingencies was difficult.

This major logistics base was well fortified since it was important for the intruders to survive. Taking out this post, therefore, became extremely crucial for the IAF.

Another pilot who still serves in the IAF was tasked to carry out an attack at this camp. 'We used the 250 kg Spanish bombs to destroy these hardened bunkers which held the enemy stores,' he tells me.

The Spanish 250 kg bomb is a very accurate weapon when dropped from a M2K as the parameters match accurately with those fed in the mission computer. These bombs were purchased on the specific recommendation of the manufacturer and proved their worth as an effective, accurate and cost-effective weapon during the conflict.

'We managed to destroy the camp at Munto Dhalo completely. With that, the sustenance of the troops ahead on the hilltops became untenable, and the Pakistani troops now knew that their end was near. We heard intercepts of their panic-stricken radio conversations with their HQ for supplies and it was clear that their logistic backbone had been severed, so vital for their survival in that area. They had no choice now, but to commence their withdrawal back into their own country.'

Another Mirage pilot who also wishes to remain anonymous told me about the difficulties of Identification Friend or Foe (IFF) during the sorties flown in the war zone. All the attacks were planned with adequate escorts so as to thwart any intervention by the fighters from the opposing side.

'In the absence of radar cover in that area, as well as poor compatibility of the different types of IFF fitted on the different aircraft flying in that area, it was pure good luck and some clear thinking on our part that prevented fratricide. The IAF and our country would have lost face if we had shot down one of our own in the fog of war,' says the pilot who flew extensively during the operations.

'We used many innovative methods so as to identify our guys. Aircraft were flying from bases as far as south as Adampur in Punjab, and although detailed briefings were carried out over the phone, there were always some grey areas.'

'One day, there was a large package of aircraft milling around Dras, and I was giving them cover from right above at 40,000 feet. As I was scanning the area for intruders on my radar, I saw two unidentified blips on my scope. To ascertain whether they were friendly, I gave a call, "All aircrafts to turn 180 degrees," I saw that all except those two turned around and obeyed my instructions.'

'I locked on to the two fellows who hadn't heeded to my call and started going towards them to carry out a visual identification, if possible, before I let go my air-to-air missiles. It turned out that that the "rogue" blips were, in fact, our own Jaguars who were not on our radio frequency channel due to some confusion. In actual combat, I would have let my missiles go as soon as they did not obey my instructions, but better sense prevailed and we prevented severe embarrassment for the country and the IAF,' says the battle-hardened pilot.

There were many such close shaves which became jokes to laugh over a drink in the evening, but on a serious note, the IAF realised that it needed to have better IFF systems, common to all aircraft on its inventory to prevent fratricide in future conflicts. Other than that, the IAF also realised that they needed to practise armament delivery and combat at high altitudes over such terrain for the future as well as integrate better with various fleets and with the Army.

Besides the Laser Guided Bomb (LGB) bombing story, about which I spoke with Namby sir, he filled me up with more of his exclusive experiences as a Mirage Pilot in the Kargil conflict.

'It is a matter of pride, honour, and satisfaction that I had the opportunity to take part in the conflict. What we train for all our lives had been achieved. If I hadn't had the opportunity, I would have gone home without having pressed a trigger, despite becoming an Air Marshal! It is almost as if I was there yesterday, walking to the aircraft with my helmet tucked under my arm, my weapon secured to my waist, my maps, authentication sheets, Pakistani currency in my pockets, and my heart thumping with excitement—all the ingredients one needed to have for an operational mission.'

'Kargil, to my mind, commenced with a major disaster. The enemy had come through our doors and was perched on our rooftops. It took the Armed Forces almost two months to evict them, losing three aeroplanes, and almost 600 lives, injuring 1,400, and the IAF lost five of our air crew. And of course, the Pakistanis took one of our pilots, Flt Lt Nachiketa, as POW.'

'We went in with a dozen M2Ks, and did things that we thought we never could or would, outside what was written in the books. Some of the boys were inducted into battle before they had even dropped a bomb from the aircraft. We were lucky to have other qualified crew who got the aircraft and the boys on line for the operations in quick time. With the best of the best servicing our aircraft, out of the 300-odd missions flown ex-Adampur, we had only three dropouts due to technical reasons. That speaks volumes about the quality of French equipment too—which, even after 20 years—performed to its full potential.'

'I always thought it was so odd to fly from a peace

station, go into war, and come back to the peace and quiet of Adampur. It is not that Adampur was not geared up for war, but as the focus was northwards, the fear of war on the western front subsided, and Adampur slipped slowly back into peacetime mode. And, ironically, at the same time, supported our operations.'

'It was so funny actually—take off from a sultry and hot Punjab in cold weather combat clothing and fight a war 400-500 km away at the icy heights. It was physiologically draining too. By the time we got airborne, the cold weather clothing we wore caused severe sweating and dehydration, leading to a fair amount of stress on our bodies.'

'We had now proven to ourselves and the country that the IAF could be brought to bear its firepower at any time, at any place of its choosing, at short notice, without really moving volumes of load from one base to the other.'

'The liaison with the Army was required at many levels and we did fairly well there too. In stark contrast to us, the Army had to move bag and baggage over rough terrain, camp in the wilderness, get acclimatised, and then fight face to face in that horrible terrain unfit for even mountain climbing.'

'Speaking of the Army, I remember a mission that we did to direct the Bofors guns firing from somewhere close to Dras. The bomb drop (point of impact) could not be sighted since the Artillery did not have their OPs (Observation Posts) in visual sight of the target area, and therefore, required someone in the air to tell them where their ammunition was landing.'

'It was at 2 am in the morning that I flew this one-of-a-kind mission over the icy mountains bathed in moonlight. It was an eerie feeling to be between the cool stars above and the ice below!'

'At 40,000 feet, I could see where the bombs were dropping on the other side. With my electro-optical infra-red system called the "Litening pod," I could aim at the bomb impact point and provide corrections to the Artillery to aim left, right, ahead, or behind. It wasn't so easy. At night, there was a lot of firing going on and it was difficult for me to see where the particular Bofors rounds were falling. So, we hit upon an idea. On my call, they would fire a tracer round which would go leaving a streak of light as it went through the air. I could now follow this round to its impact point! I realised that the shell was climbing to as high as 70,000 feet, a good 30,000 above where I was flying and then coming down over the enemy positions. It was an amusing and amazing sight at the same time to see flying missiles go right above me to their destination in the enemy camp!'

'Of course, there were problems of IFF as the other pilots must have faced too. I also had a scary encounter when I almost shot down one of ours. We had ordered that no aircraft fly below our height on a particular mission. The MiG-29s were to provide Combat Air Patrol (CAP) well above our heights and therefore, any aircraft observed below our level was to be taken as hostile for that mission.'

'I picked up a blip of one aircraft heading tangentially to us below our height and trained my sights on to it, all set to let go of my air-to-air missile. I closed in for a final check and saw that the aircraft had put its after-burners on, indicating that it was reacting to our radar pick-up and trying to get away. With my hands on the trigger, I gave one blind call on radio and after a stunned silence, the ghost aircraft announced that it was friendly. Laughable now, but at that point, it could have gone really murky.'

'The heroes of the war in the fighter class were the MiG-25s really. The MiG-25 Foxbat was bought by the IAF as a photo-intelligence gathering platform. It could fly at very high altitudes and at three times the speed of sound—making them almost "unshootable," But here, they were unarmed and tasked to carry out photo reconnaissance missions well below the heights that they regularly flew at. So, obviously, they required armed escort when they flew low and slow—sometimes as low as 400 kmph—very close to their stalling speeds at that altitude. And mind you, the MiG-25 handles very poorly at low speeds, and therefore, it was a mission requiring superior pilots with superior skills. I remember PJ Thakur, then a Wing Commander, who flew these low and slow missions, and got us very high resolution photographs which we used for bombing Tololing and other specific targets.'

'The Indian Air Force has come a long way since then. The MiG-25s lie in museums and so do so many of the planes like the Canberra, the MiG-27, and MiG-21 who flew missions in this conflict. In fact, some of us pilots who flew then are also almost ready to becoming museum pieces ourselves!'

'We have sophisticated equipment on the newer aircraft, more standoff ranges, we have better radars at those altitudes, our IFF management has improved, and so has the air defence set-up. So overall, we are much better off to fight against our enemy today as compared to those times.'

THE RUGGED AND MACHO PILOTS

GP CAPT ALOK CHAUHAN

Group Captain Alok Chauhan is a thoroughbred MiG-21 pilot. For those who don't know, the MiG 21 is an unforgiving machine and requires the best of the best to fly it, especially in combat. And the MiG-21 guys are seen as the most rugged and macho pilots who are fun loving on the ground and ruthless in the air. And that is what Squadron Leader Alok Chauhan was when he was posted to the prestigious 51 Squadron located at Srinagar in the time of the Kargil conflict.

51 Squadron was training alongside 17 Squadron at Bhatinda (Commanded by then Wing Commander BS Dhanoa who went on to become the Chief of the Air Staff later) during 1999 and was expected to stay there

till the end of May. However, on 15 May, orders were received to move back to base the very next day.

'We had a whiff of some trouble brewing, but were not expecting such a fast move,' remembers Alok, who today flies the Airbus for a commercial airline.

'Srinagar runway had been under repair and we had been operating from the nearby satellite base of Awantipora for some time before we left for Bhatinda. So, it was good to be back at home base after long,' says the veteran with many a thousand hours of flying under his belt.

Srinagar airfield was abuzz with activity when they landed. It was known that there would be action soon and the overall mood was electric. There were transport aircraft parked at all corners of the airfield and vehicles of all hues crisscrossed over the tarmac carrying loads and people in combat fatigues. This included rations, weapons and armament of all types.

'The MiG-23s and 27s had also arrived at base, and so had some MiG-29s at Awantipora. Dhanoa Sir's squadron followed us to Srinagar in a couple of days and there was a literal "mela" at the airfield,' remembers Alok, who also was the deputy flight commander of the squadron then. Friends and course mates from different squadrons interacted with each other and spoke of nothing but firing and combat.

Alok was super excited while talking to me about

the war that he took part in and the experiences of 1999 that have been etched permanently in his memory. His adrenalin spiked up as he spoke, it was as if he had just landed after a live mission.

'No one knew what the real story was and no one was asking anyone. Orders were passed down and aircraft and armament stores prepared without questions asked. In this "fog of war," I was looking for clarity of *where* we were supposed to be heading, *what* and *who* was the enemy we had to engage (targets to look for) and in what time-frame were we supposed to be ready,' says the deputy flight commander, who wanted to make sure his boys were well briefed and ready with their maps, plans, and tactics.

The media had arrived almost along with the fighting forces and were trying their best to get their 'bites' of information. Thanks to the allowed coverage, (which went a little overboard, and understandably so) this was, in fact, the first time that the Indians saw the war unfolding in front of their eyes in their bedrooms.

In a day or two, briefings were carried out and things got clearer. 'The role of my squadron was to provide Air Defence Escorts (AD ESC) to the strike formations,' says Alok. The IAF had not fired weapons at high altitudes and the Russian manuals had no data of what the ballistic figures for heights above 2.5 km (8,500 ft) were. 'All targets in the area were 14,000-15,000 feet and above and therefore, we had to get to the drawing board. Parameters of height, speed, dive angles, time of flight of weapon etc were to be recalculated.

'Tony sir (Dhanoa) and our squadron chaps worked round the clock and applied all the knowledge of weapon delivery and physics that they knew, and came up with fresh firing parameters for the heights we were expected to fire from.'

'The data from the manuals cannot be simply extrapolated from the figures available and we had to *lagao our own theta,'* (Make makeshift arrangements) says the veteran with a chuckle. A few quick dummy sorties were flown overhead Srinagar and some of the pilots were given a chance to try their hand at firing at the high altitude range of Tosha Maidan due west of the airfield.

'By and large, the weapons were hitting the targets and we were happy with our handiwork. Most of the guys had to learn on the job while doing actual missions,' he adds.

'The GPS (Global Positioning System) was new to us and we had to learn how to use the hand-held ones we were asked to share with 9 Squadron. So, I sent a few youngsters on their bikes to navigate from point to point within the airfield with the sets to learn the nitty-gritties of operating this very important piece of equipment. Once we were adept at handling the GPS, navigation to the target in the difficult area where we had to fly would be a piece of cake. The aircraft of 17 Squadron had integral GPS sets fitted and we had been envying them since they did not have to do real map reading like the rest of us! The boys were quick to learn the use of this all important navigation equipment very soon that came handy during operations.'

Use of 'map references' was also a problem area when it came to communicating with the men in green who were fighting on ground. While the army used the age-old system of 'Grid Reference', the air force used 'Coordinates' under the WGS-84 Scheme (US Standard Dept of Defence global reference system used for the GPS) adopted by all other air forces. 'This meant that we had to do a lot of minute map reading on the map references of targets given by the army—plot it on our maps and then decipher and feed it on our own systems. It was painful for the first few days, but we learnt on the go and so did the army.'

'Like I said, our job was to go along with the strike aircraft like the MiG-23s and 27s that were armed with bombs and rockets and provide them air defence cover in their immediate vicinity. The MiG-29 provided us an additional bubble of cover since they had more potent firepower and stand-off ranges.' Another set of MiG-29s and Mirage 2000s would set up a combat air patrol just ahead and above the formation. 17 Squadron had photo recce aircraft who would follow the strike and take photographs for Bomb Damage Assessment (BDA).

'So, to deliver a few 500 kg bombs and some rockets on the target, we needed a package of another eight to ten aircraft for support. We realised how important each of these were as we fought the war. In the next few days, we were to come face to face with losing aircraft and our friends to enemy fire. It was a harsh way to learn, and learn we did—for our own survival and the detriment of the enemy.'

'In anticipation of the live mission coming up, our hearts thumped, adrenalin was in full flow, and we were behaving like heroes in the action movies, capable of sorting out the bad-boys single-handedly!'

'Of course, our hearts missed a beat or two as we got into our cockpits with prayers on our lips and determination to destroy the enemy as our resolve. Our first live mission was about to begin.'

'We were wearing our overalls over brown faded *pathani* suits and special flying clothing for high altitudes. The pathani suits were required to be worn when flying over enemy territory for obvious reasons. We also carried our personal weapons strapped to our thighs along with some Pakistani currency notes. Anything was possible, and we were prepared for the worst.'

*'4 MiG-27s tasked to carry out a strike at the enemy camp at Munto Dhalo. Target—Munto Dhalo. GPS Coordinates **** Time over target 1330 hours,'* the briefing began...

'I, along with my number two were to provide escort support to the strike aircraft. We were escorting the four MiG-27 aircraft carrying the armament. Of these four-strike aircraft, two were to drop four bombs of 500 kg each while the other two were to strafe the target with rockets and their guns. Flight Lieutenant Nachiketa (nick name 'Nachi'), was the fourth in the formation doing the gun attack. Ahuja was leading the two aircraft formation who were to trail the strike by about 10 minutes and do the assessment of the battle damage by filming the area (BDA). Some helicopters were standing by for casualty evacuation at the nearby helipad under our control, should a contingency arise.'

The details of the attack plan are given in tabular format for better understanding.

'It was an intense morning and tensions were running high. We were going to go live, and it was a first for most of us. Our tough training at the academy, our flying training and experience were now going to combine into a lethal force and we were expected to "deliver" as briefed.'

'High intensity training in realistic conditions is a must to cater for drop in performance of the man behind the machine. This man also has to milk the potential of the machine to the maximum when faced with real-life, life-threatening situations. The degree of degradation of combat potential can be different for different pilots

THE DETAILS OF THE ATTACK PLAN

AC TYPE/SQN	CALLSIGN	ROLE	CREW	ARMAMENT	REMARKS
9 SQN/2 AC	BOXER ½	STRIKE	BANJO/KAT	4X500KG BOMBS	
9 SQN /2AC	HYNEA ½	STRIKE	MANDO/**NACHI**	ROCKETS/GUNS	**NACHIKETA EJECTED, POW**
51 SQN/2AC	MACHETE ½	ESCORT TO STRIKE	ALOK/SHAIKH	AIR TO AIR MISSILES/GUNS	
17 SQN/2AC	HERCULES1/2	BOMB DAMAGE ASSESSMENT	**AJAY**/BALDY	FRONT GUNS AND CAMERAS	**AJAY EJECTED, KILLED LATER BY PAKIS**
Helicopter Unit 2 helicopters	XYZ	CAS EVAC	ABC/DEF	Stretchers and medical assistants	**On call**

in differing situations, and has to be catered for. As the squadron pilots at this frontline base got used to flying more operational missions in the days ahead, this combat degradation had come down by many a notch.'

However, this was the first mission.

'The aircraft got airborne as planned. The first two MiG-27s dropped their bombs and returned to base. From that height, one could see small mushroom clouds of dust rising from where they impacted. Bombs were on target!'

One can only imagine how it is at the receiving end of the bomb. The sound is deafening, splinters and rocks fly like missiles and the blast sucks in the air around asphyxiating everyone. The shock waves can be felt for miles around.

'It was time for Nachiketa and his leader, Mando to let go of their rockets. Rockets have to be aimed and fired at the target from closer ranges. Unfortunately, Mando could not see the target as he got into the dive and aborted his attack. Nachi, who was following, had contact with the target and went in for the attack letting go a lethal spray of rockets and turned around for another go.'

'Confirm contact with target, look for my weapon impact,' radioed Nachi to Mando. Mando replied in the affirmative and followed Nachi who was going in for his second pass. Mando let go of his rockets and Nachi came in for one final pass over the target with his front guns, asking Mando to follow him.

Suddenly, the radio crackled to life, 'I have an engine failure, attempting relight...' said Nachiketa, his voice calm as a cucumber. He had turned away from the target and gained height with extra speed. Mando followed him, trying to see if he would come out of the situation.

'No joy, Ejecting!' boomed Nachiketa's voice over the radio. The next minute, Mando saw the aircraft go into a rapid descent and crash into a plume of dust and flame. He could not see any parachute deploying, and thought that the worst had happened. Nachi had gone down with the airplane. After a few more orbits to look for his buddy, and low on fuel, he set course for Srinagar hoping for a miracle.

In the words of the Escort leader, Alok, 'We had set up orbit over the MiG-27s as they went about their business. The terrain was so jagged and undulating below and I was wondering how the guys were even able to sight the target in the first place. We were flying well above the envelope of the shoulder-fired missiles, but these guys were definitely within range. There seemed to be no enemy air activity in the vicinity, and therefore, we were safe from above, at least.'

'Before Nachi went down, I had seen a few plumes of smoke emanating from the ground that appeared to be shoulder-fired missiles. I warned about the same to the aircraft below. In fact, some of those projectiles came up right till our heights. Probably, the manufacturers had not calculated that the weapon would travel much higher in the rarefied atmosphere! Later, when the historians wrote about the conflict, I read that as many as 38 missiles were fired at us on Day-One of the war.'

The escort formation, low on fuel, returned to Srinagar.

'On the way back, we got in touch with Squadron Leader Ajay Ahuja, the formation leader of the bomb damage assessment (BDA) mission-call-sign "Hercules."' Ajay was an accomplished pilot and the flight commander of 17 Squadron. Displaying the highest qualities of leadership, he had put himself as the mission leader for the first mission from his squadron. The conversation between the two formations 'Machete' and 'Hercules' went something like this:

M: Hercules 1 from Machete 1.

H: Go ahead, Machete 1.

M: Shoulder-fired missile threat over the target area. Exercise caution and do not descend below prescribed height.

H: Roger, Check position of Hyena-2?

M: Hynea-2 crashed near target area, Nachi gave a call ejecting, chute not sighted.

H: Roger.

M: Happy shooting. Over and out.

'We landed back in Srinagar where there was general

confusion as to who had gone down. They asked me if Hercules 1 had crashed. I explained and reiterated to them that I had seen Hyena-2 crash and crossed Hercules formation on way back. I was wrong there. Hercules-1 also had crashed in the intervening period. I dashed to the ops room after landing to check what the real news was.'

The situation update was that Ajay had ejected, and his parachute had been seen. 'I hoped he had landed on our side of the border and would be picked up by our chopper soon enough. I prayed that Nachi too had survived and possibly we hadn't seen his chute deploy.'

By the evening, the news had been confirmed. Nachiketa had been taken as POW and would return after a few weeks in captivity. He had been captured after landing by a Captain of the Pakistani Army who had prevented his men from bludgeoning him to death. He had actually fired from his pistol when they surrounded him and could have been shot by the Pakis, but thankfully, they let him be. As soon as the nine rounds of his Makarov pistol were exhausted, they overpowered him and took him into captivity. What happened to him is another story, which, maybe, Nachi may tell us after a few years.

After his filming run, Ajay decided to orbit around the crash site to look for his comrade Nachiketa. He orbited there for long enough and drifted down to get a better look. At this point in time, a shoulder-fired missile was launched at his aircraft which managed to, most probably, damage his jet-pipe leading to reduction of thrust.

He gave a call that his engine had lost power before he ejected, and radioed his coordinates of where he was ejecting, so that it would be easy for the chopper to pick him up. Pulling his ejection handle, he was out of the sick aircraft in a flash. Soon his chute deployed, and he started floating down, drifting with the wind. Unfortunately for him, he finally touched ground on the enemy side.

Ajay wasn't so lucky as Nachi. As he descended into enemy territory, he was fired upon by the Mujahids in all probability. It is said that Ahuja started firing back at the enemy well before he had touched the ground using his pistol.

When his body arrived in Srinagar later, all those who saw him realised that he had been fired upon from close quarters. He had one bullet through his heart and one through his temple, meaning that he had been killed at point blank range after landing safely on ground.

It is against the Geneva conventions and not fair to shoot a pilot coming down on his parachute—but then, who said war is fair? In fact, the captain of the Pakistan army who had saved Nachiketa from certain death was later killed in one of our bombings a few days later.

The air force was just about getting out of the shock of losing two aircraft on the first day of the war. Just a couple of days later, our Mi-17 piloted by Squadron Leader Pundir and Flt Lt Muhilan was shot in the same area.

After the three crashes, and the loss of five lives—Ajay and the four crew of the Mi-17, the IAF had learnt valuable lessons on fighting in high altitude terrain against a well-entrenched enemy. The war continued for the next few weeks and the guns finally fell silent on 26 July, 1999.

'Did you think the war would escalate?' I ask him.

'We were fighting a war with a well-entrenched enemy and it was going to be difficult to evict them from the vantage positions that they had taken over. So, the feeling that we got was that it would be a long-drawn battle, and therefore, the chances were that it would escalate. We also felt that the enemy would probably draw us into a battle in other sectors so as to ease the pressure up north.'

During the conflict, the Indian side had to exercise extreme restraint to ensure that they did not cross the LOC and cause embarrassment to the government.

The logistical issues were really enormous. Road move of stores to the Kashmir valley takes a lot of time. It was our transport planes who flew day in and day out to get in the armament which we would expend as soon as they were unpacked and made ready for use. A lot of innovations were also achieved during this time. The GPS kit was modified to be fitted on to a 'dumb' bomb so as to make it reach the target. Kudos to the technical staff and the test pilots who worked ceaselessly while we fought the battle.

'And while we fought the battle, the media and the celebrities also did a fine job of keeping our morale up. The people on ground were kept entertained by the singers and celebrities who also signed their messages on the bombs being dropped on the enemy! The media also showed that they could help fight the war alongside us.'

When I asked him about his last thoughts on Kargil, he replied, 'With the passage of time, the IAF has reconsidered how it would fight in the mountains, something that you have seen in the recent flare-up with the Chinese.'

'In my opinion, conventional war is almost impossible today and we have to prepare for high intensity-high tempo operations in localised areas from now on. For this, we have to optimise our weaponry and equipment as also our tactics. The use of high-end technology and the ability to strike with precision is the name of the game.'

'Last, but not the least, synergy between the three services needs to improve, we need to fight together as one unit and speak the same language. We also need to become more pro-active rather than reactive in our approach to fighting.'

'These aspects have been improving, but we still have a long way to go. And yes, we need to have our diplomacy tuned up to search for solutions before things go the military way.'

I ask him my last queston, 'What about your families? How did they live in constant tension?'

'I think I will write and tell you about it,' said Alok, and we said our good bye.

As promised, I received a mail from the veteran which is reproduced below:

> Servicemen around the world go off to their deployments and leave their loved ones behind. It is a poorly recognised fact what role they—the loved ones—play in clarity of thought and purpose of the individual at risk. Actually, in hindsight, the soldier isn't at risk at all. Actually, it is the loved ones who are at risk of losing their bread-winner.
>
> The enormity of this simple fact came to light when my wife Arti decided that she had to be with me during the Ops as they started. It was her first time in Srinagar and made worse by the fact that we did not have accommodation, thanks to our previous deployment in Awantipora (that's where our baggage was too), but then she would have none of it and she was on the last flight into Srinagar before ops commenced, with my eight-month-old son.

We put up in a single room of a two-bedroom flat offered by another bachelor who moved in with his friend.

The initial days were tough since I was never available to even pick up basic necessities like milk or baby food for home. I was never there at breakfast or lunch or for that matter sometimes dinner too. But then, she could call me at will, walking to the nearest phone, baby in tow. Never did I hear her even whisper to me about the problems she was facing, as she struggled to happily provide for us within almost non-existent resources.

Of course, her rationale was pretty simple as she put it—she would rather be acutely aware and involved rather than speculate as to what was happening. A fact that stood her in good stead when she had heard of my ejection at treetop height about five years ago.

Of course, as ops progressed, there came a time when you needed to lay down facts. What if I didn't return from a mission? And there wasn't much to go by, if it did happen. She always replied to it with a smile, 'We shall see but for now, focus on what you need to do.'

It was therefore easier for me, to go into conflict in my supersonic jet, to face hostility, just a short distance from her and know that she will be able to take care of things if they went wrong. It gave me an edge, to fly with sharp focus, clarity and enhanced awareness.

The evenings during the ops were spent with friends with a lot of stories and laughter thrown in to lighten the mood. But the hidden fact is—as I went up again and again, it was her who was smilingly sending me off every day with a cheerful 'See ya,' and she did so knowing the risk that could potentially leave her and my son alone for life and with a paltry sum of just over a lakh in savings and bureaucratic government support.

It then dawned on me that it was not only me who was fighting the war.

I tell you, mutual love, understanding, and that 'couples therapy' that the Air Force gave me made the toughest and trying times look tame.

BIRTHDAY CAKE AND MISSILES

WG CDR SHAKUL TYAGI

My friend from Army Aviation, Colonel R (who doesn't want to be named) long retired but a keen helicopter buff, narrated me this story when I told him I was writing a piece on helicopter operations in Kargil.

'There were marks in the snow as I carried out a helicopter recce of the areas we had withdrawn from during the winters. This was almost a year before the actual fighting broke out. I had gone there with three of my aircraft for my annual training in which we practised "shoots" with the artillery.'

'I sensed that things were not right since the artillery guns were not available for practice for live firing at the ranges. There had been sporadic firing from across, which was getting more and more accurate, and our artillery was being readied for counter bombardment. We also saw the place near Dras and Kargil that was bombed. It appeared that the Pakistani gunners were getting accurate inputs on the "fall of shot," and that could happen only if they were visual with the Indian side.'

'On a special reconnaissance flight along the Dras-Kargil axis, we saw fresh footprints in the snow at the posts vacated by our soldiers for the winters. Putting two and two together, it was evident that the Pakistanis had infiltrated on to our side and were well dug in already. I submitted a written report of my findings and went back to my base.'

'I guess it was taken too casually then, if we had acted on the inputs, Kargil would not have happened. But that is conjecture!'

Helicopters always have been a very important part of any mission, offensive or otherwise. And so were they in Kargil. By 10-11 May, around eight helicopters of the Mi-17 class had been inducted into Srinagar. A large number of troops, ammunition, and stores were transported in and the para-commandos were being given refresher training to slither from the helicopters.

All the aircrew had been called to discuss options at a meeting held in the underground Operations Centre at Srinagar which continued well into the night. Targets were at extreme heights, accuracy as well as aircraft limitations were issues and discussions heated up as the night wore on.

'Nana Menon (Air Officer Commanding Jammu and Kashmir) and Air Marshal Vinod Patney (Air Officer Commanding-in-chief Western Air Command) were also present along with one Lieutenant General from the Army, and gave a patient hearing to all,' says Wing Commander Shakul Tyagi, who had the privilege of being there at Srinagar right through the operations and through whose eyes I describe this story on helicopter operations in Kargil.

'For the first time we saw that the fighter boys spoke about the high efficacy and efficiency of the helicopters in an armed role in this scenario. I was happy and proud to hear that the importance of helicopters as a weapon platform was being recognised by the fighter boys,' says the veteran who now flies in the Civvy Street.

The MiG-27 had severe problems of weapon release at high altitude and it was opined that the engine may fail due to the high thrust and blast of the weapons at that altitude. Finally, the big bosses took the decision. The fighters were to give supporting fire and help in keeping the enemy heads down and as soon as they did their bit, the helicopters were to spring a surprise on them by carrying out rocket attacks at the posts on the hill tops. A well co-ordinated operation was the need of the hour.

The question of shoulder-fired missiles also came

up during these discussions. All the helicopters were not equipped with flare-firing equipment to thwart the shoulder-fired Stingers which the enemy was known to have in plenty. A via media was worked out, each attacking the formation of four helicopters was to have at least two fitted with the equipment and helicopters were to fly in close proximity of each other till they fired at the target. This was to prove fatal just a few days later.

'When we discussed tactics and details amongst ourselves, we concluded that we would fire our rockets and dive into the valley and get away, making it difficult for the enemy to fire their missiles at us. Also, we decided to do the morning missions from the east with the sun behind us so that we could be hidden in the glare. The evening missions were, of course to be done from the west. That was the best way to keep safe.'

'If the fighters were raw at firing at those altitudes, we hadn't had any exposure at all, and therefore, we were at a huge disadvantage. But helicopter pilots are innovative and quick to adapt to new situations and tactics and we did so and put everyone's doubts about us to rest.'

'A total of five missions by four aircraft each were flown by us, the first one being on the morning of 26 May. On the first day, things went as planned but for the aircraft with CMDS (Counter Measure Dispensing System) which had some technical snag. We had an army observer in the lead aircraft who tried to identify targets for us.'

Perspectives change with height and it was difficult for the army observer to orientate himself in the air. But with some help from the pilots, he did manage fairly well.

'On the way back, we landed at the helipad at Mattayan to pick up casualties. It was here that we got a debrief from the artillery boys who had observed the firing from where they were deployed. We did two successful missions that day—the same day that we lost the two fighters and got the news of Ahuja's killing.'

'In fact, both the fighters went down within 45 minutes of each other and we were told to hastily prepare for a Combat Search and Rescue mission, (CSAR), something that we had only practiced little. We, of course, had read of the daring missions flown by the USAF to pick up their downed pilots from behind enemy lines in Afghanistan and Iraq.'

Despite the fact that this was to be the most dangerous of missions with every chance of not coming back, all the aircrew volunteered for the mission with Wing Commander AK Sinha, the overall task force commander leading from the front. They were loaded with 192 rockets, bullet proof jackets, emergency stores and their personal weapons to go within an hour of being told to get ready.

'With heavy hearts, we saw the aircraft taking off that morning, we knew that there was a good chance of casualties. But, as they took off, the ATC radioed them to return. News had been received from across the border that Ahuja was dead and Nachi was in their hands.

'Similar armament delivery missions were flown on 27 July, the targets being Tololing Top and a place called Helmet Feature. These were successful and we were gaining in both, confidence and marksmanship.'

'We also flew one big 130 mm Medium Gun (7,700 kgs) broken up in three parts and slung under the aircraft from Kupwara to Balbir Top where it was urgently required on that day. These Russian 'Medium' guns have a 30 plus km range and proved to be very accurate weapons during this conflict. Besides this, six light guns were dropped in the Gurez Valley to augment firepower on the same day.'

Shifting from an offensive role to a load-carrying role is not easy. Ask the technical guys and they will tell you what a back-breaking effort it is. Pylons and pods have to be removed, rollers and load carrying boards need to be fitted, the rear doors need to be removed for drop sorties plus some electrical and hydraulic connections need change.

Young Flight Lieutenant Jamuar, who headed the technical team, needs a special mention here. He used to get up at 0230 at night and go to the aircraft. Eating all his meals on the tarmac, he preferred to be with his men and provide them the motivation to work round the clock. He more often than not, got just a few hours in his bed for days on end.

'We flew all these missions seeing enemy shells landing around us, it was scary, quite uncomfortable but unforgettable!'

On 27th evening, Squadron Leader Pundir arrived from the parent base at Sarsawa (Saharanpur) in an An-32 aircraft as additional crew. He got along a cake for Flight Lieutenant Muhilan from his wife Bina. Muhilan's birthday was coming up in the next two days and celebrations were in the offing.

'The cake was kept on the table near the bed. Muhilan and I shared the room,' remembers the veteran.

The birthday bash was to be after the mission on 28 July. The morning mission on 28th was with Wing Commander Anil Kumar Sinha (Chinky) Sir, (now veteran Air Cmde Anil Kumar Sinha) in the lead and Pundir and Muhilan as No 3. 'While the aircrafts started up in the morning, there was a lot of panic on the tarmac with two helicopters going unserviceable.' Crew hopped from one helicopter to another and finally the mission got airborne. There had been an inordinate delay which was going to prove costly.

Meanwhile, the fighters, who were going to give them fire support, got airborne as planned and did their jobs. They were returning to base, low on fuel, when the helicopters reached to fire their rockets.

The helicopters flew tucked in close to each other as

decided so as to get cover from the missile threat. Two aircraft dispensed their flares as they descended into the missile envelope of the enemy, closing in to the target. But when it was time to fire, the helicopters had to maintain lateral separation from each other so that they did not fly into each other's wake or trajectory. This was the opportunity that the enemy with the shoulder-fired missiles on ground were waiting for.

A missile was fired, and good luck favoured the Pakistanis for a change. The missile scored a direct hit. The aircraft flown by Pundir and Muhilan went spiralling down and crashed into a plume of dust and smoke. There was no hope for the crew.

'It was a sad ending to a series of successes. But then, in war, one has to bear losses too, and we did take it in our stride. The helicopter operations came to a stop till we got our CMDS (Counter Measures Dispensing System) aircraft on line.' By then, the Army had already claimed back our territory losing almost 500+ lives and more than double that number injured.

Operation 'Safed Sagar,' as it was aptly named, came to an end by mid-July, and the guns officially fell silent on 26 July with Prime Minister Vajpayee announcing complete eviction of the Pakistani intruders.

The untouched cake kept on Muhilan's bedside kept reminding me of my roommate—a stark reminder of the cruelty of war.

Acknowledgements

I have often found that the greatest books ever written are not an assortment of words and themes randomly put together, but stories that people relate to, or are awed by. On closer inspection, I feel that very often well written stories are, in reality, accounts of lives well lived.

If I start counting my fortune for the sheer number of people I have come across who have lived their lives well, I might end up filling this entire book with their names. But there are a few whose lives have defined the pages of history. Those whose courage and presence of mind have possibly saved thousands of lives and saved the red blob from turning to brown. It was this motive of recording history as well as speaking to the people who made it, that I set out to write articles for *rediff.com* on the 1971 Liberation War and the Kargil conflict. Little did I know that these stories would later take the shape of a book.

These stories come straight from the hearts of soldiers who fought gallantly against the enemy despite all odds that they faced in the fog of war. To those who lost their lives in protecting our freedom, the nation salutes them for their ultimate sacrifice.

But during the process of writing these stories, there are a few people who made my life easier.

My deepest gratitude to Mr Nikhil Lakshman, Editor-in-Chief, *rediff.com* to allow me to use the articles for the book. And to Ms Renu Kaul Verma, Managing Director, Vitasta Publishing, for taking this idea forward. To the editors at Vitasta, especially Alisha, you had a very difficult task at hand—to weave these stories into a flow. Thank you for being my glim lamps.

Each story that I got from the Armed Forces veterans felt like a sneaky peek into the annals of history. I knew what had transpired but I didn't know the *how*. Lucid in the recollections of events, these stories gave me a 'behind the scene' glimpse of war. There stories made me squeal with awe, respect and worry as if I was an eight year-old on a train, seeing the world pass by me for the first time. No measure of gratitude and thanks will be enough to the soldiers who let me in their homes, inboxes, hearts and minds. But for all that it counts... Thank you, Veterans, not just for sharing your stories, but also for the great service you have done and the legacy you are leaving the younger generations with. This book, literally and figuratively, would not be possible without you.

Thank you for answering the thousand questions I had. You have made every Indian proud and your stories will continue to motivate and inspire many Indians who look at what the military does in awe.

Last, but not the least, my gratitude and love to my near and dear ones, my friends and my numerous readers who have always inspired me to write.

I can be reached out at palnits@yahoo.com and at facebook.com/nitin.sathe.7146. Will be waiting eagerly for your reviews!